My Life in the Wild

My Life in the Wild

Ivan Tors

Illustrated with Photographs

Houghton Mifflin Company   Boston 1979

Library of Congress Catalog Card Number:

Tors, Ivan.
   My life in the wild.

      1. Tors, Ivan.   2. Zoologists — United States —
Biography.   3. Moving-picture producers and directors —
United States — Biography.   I. Title.
QL31.T59A37   591'.092'4   79-12252
ISBN 0-395-27766-3

Printed in the United States of America

s 10 9 8 7 6 5 4 3 2 1

I dedicate this book to my teachers, friends, and companions around the world, and to my three African sons.

SOUTHERN AFRICA
Ian Player, Makubu, and Nick Steele (Zululand, Natal, S.A.); Jan Oelofse (Namibia; Kruger National Park, Transvaal, S.A.); Terry Reille (Swaziland); Sven Persson (South Africa; Mozambique); Jimmy Chapman (Zululand, Natal, S.A.; Kruger National Park, Transvaal, S.A.); Hank Maartens (Rhodesia).

EAST AFRICA
John Pearson (Tanzania; Kenya, Uganda); Simon Trevor (Tsavo National Park, Kenya; Ngorongoro Crater, Tanzania); Jack Hopcraft (Great Rift Valley, Kenya); Don Hunt (Mount Kenya, Kenya); Reggie Destro (Chalbi Desert, Lake Turkana, and Great Rift Valley, Kenya); Murray Watson (Masai Mara Game Reserve and Laikipia, Kenya); Tony Harthoorn, John Seago, and Tony Parkinson (Samburu Game Reserve and Tsavo National Park, Kenya).

SOUTH ASIA
Percy De Alwis (Komodo Island, Indonesia; Bangalore, India; Sri Lanka).

AUSTRALIA
Ben and Eva Cropp (Great Barrier Reef); David Brown (Queensland).

CENTRAL AND SOUTH AMERICA
Ramon Bravo (Costa Rica); Stan Brock (Orinoco River, Venezuela).

FLORIDA AND THE ISLANDS
John Lilly (Virgin Islands); Ricou Browning (Florida; Bahamas); Courtney Brown (Fort Lauderdale, Florida); Willie Meyers (Bahamas).

UNDERWATER COMPANIONS
Zale Parry, Parry Bivens, Lamar Boren, Jordan Klein, Francis D. Fane.

OTHER TEACHERS AND FRIENDS
L. S. B. Leakey (Kenya); Phil Tobias (University of Witwatersrand, South Africa); Robert Ardrey (Capetown); Fred White (UCLA and Scripps Institution of Oceanography, California); and all the game guards and native guides who shared with me their great knowledge and understanding of wildlife.

Contents

My Life in the Wild

1 Introduction

I CONSIDER IT A MIRACLE that at sixty-two I am still alive and a United States citizen. Statistically, I did not have a chance of survival. Yet I feel healthy, vigorous, and young.

I was born in the midst of a famine during World War I; and I escaped from my native Hungary six weeks before the outbreak of World War II and Hungary's joining forces with Hitler.

I came to the United States originally to study, but soon I started writing in Hollywood and met people like Garbo, Stravinsky, and Rubinstein. When America entered the war, I joined the American Air Force and was later recruited into the OSS.

After the war, MGM hired me as a contract writer, and I wrote films for Katharine Hepburn, Judy Garland, Greer Garson, and Errol Flynn. I met most of the big stars, directors, and moguls of that unreal world.

In 1950 I started to produce my own films. I had a good scientific background and had always been interested in world geography, so it was not coincidental that my films took me on expeditions to faraway places and into the realms of science and science fiction.

I went on scuba diving expeditions with Navy frogmen and worked with space scientists and oceanographers who explored both inner and outer space. Among the visionaries I knew and respected were J. B. Rhine, L. S. B. Leakey, Aldous Huxley, John Lilly, and Charles Lindbergh.

My nature series and my animal encyclopedia took me on many field trips — forty times to Africa and three times around the world — to study the elegant society of the African elephant, the primitive world of the alligators in the Everglades and of the Nile crocodiles, and the wild herds of the African antelope.

I lived among the Camel People of Africa when a seven-year drought littered their sand dunes with skeletons. I swam among sharks off Australia and in the Caribbean. I followed the migration of the whales and befriended killer whales. I collected venomous snakes and learned that they were far from dangerous. I nearly lost my life in the South Pacific when a current swept me away from the Navy ship from which I was diving. Luckily, a Navy lookout spotted me, in a state of exhaustion, a mile from the boat. Another time, my life was saved by the dolphin who later became famous as Flipper.

I was assigned to capture forty-seven tiger sharks for the motion picture *Thunderball*. For the same film I had to swim in a pool filled with sharks to prove to Sean Connery that sharks are not really aggressive unless in a feeding frenzy.

While I was flying over Zululand at an altitude of 9000 feet, the cargo hatch suddenly opened and I found myself hanging from the plane. For a good sixty seconds I clung to the hatch door, upsetting the balance of the aircraft. Another time I flew through a hurricane between Panama and Columbia in a small Cessna without a radio. And during a hurricane in Miami, the roof of the room in which I was sleeping took off like a giant kite.

I introduced six hundred wild animals such as lions, tigers, leopards, and buffalo to California, where our company owned a beautiful valley. I had learned from mother dolphins that young animals respond warmly to the human touch, and so almost all of these animals were touched every day. I called this "affection training." It seemed that our loving touch became more important than food to the animals, and I coined the phrase, "There is no love without touching."

I became adept at hypnosis. I treated sick tribesmen and sometimes healed people by my touch — I don't know how! I became a guru to many. In Kenya I am called M'Zee, which means "the wise one." I suppose my white beard is largely responsible for that.

Working with animals, I became interested in nonverbal communication, ESP, precognition, out-of-body experiences, and all psychic phenomena. I developed a theory of biocommunication, a system that connects all living things with each other, and presented it to the Society of Psychic Research and the Menninger Foundation. My theory has not yet been refuted.

I lectured at medical seminars on the immobilization of wildlife with dart guns and psychopharmacology, and on stress in the animal world. I learned a great deal from Dr. Hans Selye, the father of the stress syndrome, who believed that there is a

"Affection training" a llama (*Metro-Goldwyn-Mayer*)

condition of sickness and a condition of health and that disease is a symptom that shows us our natural immune systems are not in harmony.

I became a behaviorist. At the University of California at Irvine I was appointed lecturer in psychiatry and human behavior. At that time I was the only non–M.D. on the faculty. Later I received my Master's Degree in zoology for my field studies on animal guidance systems.

I was fortunate enough to see wildlife as it really was. The animals and I became good friends. I respected their living space, never threatened them with weapons, and they never threatened me, either, unless provoked.

As a result of my work, I have lost all of the human arrogance that allowed me to feel superior to the creatures of the wild — I believe we are only different from them. An elephant can have as much compassion for her child as a human, even more so. At the Maputo Game Reserve in Mozambique, a game guard observed a mother elephant with a mutilated trunk. A poacher's snare had cut off the end of her trunk so that she was unable to feed herself. She would have been condemned to slow death by starvation had not her year-old baby saved her life by uprooting vegetation with her own small trunk and placing the food in her mother's mouth. This kind of cooperation reflects love, intelligence, and a true communication between mother and child, for it is not an established genetic behavior pattern for a baby to feed her mother. Yes, humans are different, but how different? And are they better?

Most animals evolved through eons of time into their final forms. Lions, tigers, elephants, rhinos, hippos, leopards, baboons, and crocodiles looked very much the same many million years ago as they look today. Insects, fish, and simpler life forms may not have changed at all in fifty million to five hundred million years. But civilized man is at the very beginning of his life cycle. Agriculture and writing are less than ten thousand years old. Our bodies keep changing; the human species is constantly growing in size. Why, then, are we more cruel and destructive than nearly all animal species? Do we deserve to survive when we are constantly destroying our environment (something very few animals do, and only when their migration is thwarted because of roads, fences, and other human pressures)?

Animals are very important to me. Constantly they teach me what they know best: the secrets of survival, proper care for the young, the importance of cooperation, the right and urge to defend territories, the functions of the male and the female. Even the feared shark, seemingly immune to most infections, may teach us some medical secrets. No animal is useless.

All species evolved to fill a void. For every circumstance, a different animal has been created by natural selection. A good example is the giraffe, which, with the longest neck in the animal kingdom, can feed on the top of the umbrella tree, so that this vegetation does not go to waste. Even the worm is necessary for softening the soil; the snake, to keep destructive rodents in balance.

It seems to me that man, too, evolved to serve a purpose in this cosmos. He developed a large brain so that he could understand this purpose. I try to understand the human species by studying nature's way and my animal friends.

Let me introduce you to some of my best friends.

2 The Elegant Killers

I T I S D A Y B R E A K in the savanna. All around are termite mounds, thorn bushes, acacia trees, and short yellow grass. The land is flat. The night is cold, and the grass eaters come out of the bushes to warm themselves as the sun slowly rises. Small herds of Thompson gazelles and the taller, more statuesque Grant gazelles, with their delicate limbs of ballerinas, emerge. There are some impalas grazing at a distance, and the larger wildebeests move across the horizon in a herd. An ungainly wart hog mama rises from her hole and four little piglets follow her with tails standing straight up like four little flagpoles. All these grass eaters are being observed by the most elegant hunter of Africa, the cheetah. The cheetah is the fastest land mammal we know of, and her spotted coat blends with the vegetation. She is hiding three little cubs in the brush behind her and they already know that they must stay put if they intend to survive. Baby cheetahs do not look like cheetahs at all. A grayish mane covers them down to the tail. Only their bellies and feet are yellow and spotted. This camouflage offers them protection against hyenas, jackals, and eagles who love to feed on young cheetahs when the mother is away. I watch her from my hiding place. She knows that I am there and by now she is used to me and accepts me as a harmless creature from outer space about whom she no longer has to be concerned.

The strange grace of a cheetah (*Photo by John Pearson*)

Mama is very skinny. The three young cubs have sucked out all the nutrients stored in her body. It is dawn and her time to hunt.

I am watching her through my strong binoculars. Suddenly I see her motionless, statuelike, on the top of a yellow brown termite mound. She scans the surrounding savanna and sights her prey. She slides off the mound. What I am watching now is nature's cruel way. Or is it cruel? A flesh eater will attempt to kill a grass eater to produce nutrition for herself and her offspring. I watch her stride; she walks cautiously but without anxiety. Even her walk is different from other felines. Her claws are not retractable like the claws of the rest of the cat world. Possibly, she is the missing link between the family of dogs and cats. Her body is built for speed, with long tapering legs and a powerful chest. She has a small mouth but very strong teeth. The two tear lines, two black stripes running from her eyes to the corners of her mouth, also mark her distinction from other big cats.

She has picked a grazing herd of Thompson gazelles. Now

she approaches them and moves from bush to bush like a commando or guerrilla ready for a sudden attack. Some of the gazelles become anxious and nervous. They sense danger. But one of them does not pay much attention. Probably she is the most sluggish and retarded of the lot, the weakest link in the gene pool of this herd, and she will be the one to be killed and eaten.

The cheetah crouches, never taking her eyes off the unsuspecting gazelle. Then she breaks into a run, and soon she is at top speed, probably sixty miles per hour. The gazelle tries to evade her, but to no avail. The gazelle is knocked over by the impact of the charge and, as she falls, the cheetah's teeth are fastened to her throat. Death comes fast and painlessly. The stamina of the cheetah lasts only for a spurt of about three hundred yards, and now her chest heaves from the exertion. Breathing heavily, she lets her dead prey out of her grasp for a few moments, to recover. Then she slowly begins to drag the gazelle toward the bush from where her three infants have been watching the kill.

The cheetah pulls the gazelle under the cover of the thorn bush and begins to feed on the buttock. The babies are still on milk and are not interested in meat, but they enjoy bathing in the warm blood. They lick each other's funny faces; they lick the mother's bloody nose and prance around the carcass, learning about the anatomy of the prey. Then they play tug of war with the intestines. One of the infants seems to be weaker than the others. Mother will pick her up in her mouth and carry her as they move from bush to bush.

Once the young are weaned, the mother will have to make a kill every morning to keep them alive. Nine months from now they'll be ready to hunt like commandos, in a staggered line, stalking gazelles behind bushes and attacking on a signal from their mother.

My three young sons were often with me to witness such kills and we seldom found it cruel. Death comes fast and any sympathy for the gazelle is often outweighed by sympathy for the hungry young cheetahs.

I have tremendous respect for cheetahs. Full grown they weigh only 100 to 130 pounds, and they must survive among predators much stronger than themselves, such as prides of lions and the most professional killer of all, the leopard, who likes to kill cheetahs because he considers them competition. Hyenas and jackals often try to steal away the cheetahs' kills and martial eagles swoop down out of the sky to pick off the cheetahs' young. Still they show caution only, not anxiety. They look at men with fearless contempt. Somehow, they have made their peace with humans. They have often allowed me to follow them closely, and on one occasion a cheetah looking for shade to ingest a Grant gazelle she had just killed, found cover under our Land-Rover.

A friend of mine wrote a book about an orphaned cheetah he saved when he was working as a game guard in Botswana. The cheetah paid him back later by saving his life when my friend was attacked by a leopard. The cheetah, jumping on the leopard's back, surprised the killer and gave my friend a chance to get away unhurt. After this experience, he became obsessed with cheetahs, and when he married a woman who owned a farm, he decided to train cheetahs there. One day I received a call from him some six hundred miles away. He explained that he had six cheetahs he had brought up from infancy and they had become so obedient and well trained that he felt I must make a film about them. So I drove the six hundred miles with my sons to what could be called The House of Cheetahs.

Cheetahs were everywhere — six adults with their lovely infants. The owner immediately tried to demonstrate to me how well trained his cheetahs were — a demonstration that turned out to be a complete failure. When he said, "Come here," the cheetah sat down; when he told him to "sit down," the cheetah walked away. They were *tame* all right, but *trained* — no. All cheetahs have a will of their own, just like most house cats. In my experience with the cat family, the two most difficult species to train are the cheetah and the house cat. Give me a lion or a tiger any time — you can bribe them to do anything, just as house dogs will. But cheetahs are unique.

In 1964 when I became a board member of the World Wildlife Fund, cheetahs did not breed in captivity and they were on the endangered species list. Since then, zoological parks have had success in breeding programs by using more territory and sex hormone treatments. So I, too, decided to breed cheetahs, at Africa USA, giving them plenty of ground with good grass. I acquired six or seven cheetahs. Now and then one escaped and we would bring him back by lassoing him. The cheetahs did not at all like being dragged back on a rope, nor being manhandled, so they would snarl and look threatening. Still, not one ever tried to bite me when I brought him back to his enclosure. When they do not like you, they try to avoid you, but very seldom does a cheetah attack his keeper.

On the other hand, for some reason they hate all horses. When riding on the farm, I have noticed that they never take their eyes off our mounts. Once an escaped cheetah even attacked my horse while I was riding. The horse reared in fright and fell with me into the lake where we keep alligators and crocodiles. My cameraman was there to get the shot and we later used the scene under the main title of the MGM picture *Rhino*. No one knew that I was the fierce stuntman on the runaway horse — or how scared I was.

My good friend Stan Brock, the cohost of *Wild Kingdom*, nearly got killed in Rhodesia while catching a cheetah with a throw net from a horse. Stan, who was once a *vaquero* in the Amazon jungle, is a great cowboy and he seldom misses. He caught the cheetah on the first try. Then the director suggested that he do it again just to be sure that they had two takes. The cheetah was let go again and Stan tried to repeat the stunt, but this time the cheetah knew what to expect. He avoided the net, jumped on top of the horse, and bit Stan's face just under his eyes. Stan was nearly killed. He was flown to

Johannesburg where a great plastic surgeon saved his eyesight and restored his face.

Still, even this cheetah was willing to forget the grudge. When not bothered again, it displayed no hostility toward us, and my son Peter later made friends with it.

Cheetahs are aristocratic in both appearance and attitude— dignified loners, champions. Further evidence of this comes from an account in the *Guinness Book of Animal Facts and Feats*. In 1937 an Englishman bought six cheetahs in Kenya. He tried to race them against the fastest greyhounds in England. Although a cheetah is not very trainable, it will chase a hare by instinct, even if the hare is artificial and runs electrically. The cheetahs beat the greyhounds easily, but strange as it may seem, the cheetahs were never hostile toward the greyhounds, while the greyhounds were hostile toward the cheetahs. When the hounds attacked them, the cheetahs did not retaliate. They merely cuffed the greyhounds the way they would cuff a misbehaving pup.

Of all the big cats, I like tigers the best, but I respect cheetahs the most. Anyone who poaches a cheetah for its magnificent pelt is no friend of mine, and I would willingly do to him what he does to the cheetah.

I learned a great deal about ecology and the so-called balance of nature from cheetahs — things I could never learn from my zoology books. We considered the cheetah near extinction in East Africa and placed it on the endangered list because its numbers had been so depleted by poachers and lions. To avoid the predatory lion, cheetahs seek arid, low grass areas with scanty bushes, where lions cannot find enough shade and sufficient hideaways. Lions are very territorial creatures. They mark their boundaries with urine and resent having other predators, including leopards, in their domain. But leopards live in trees, so lions cannot easily chase them away. Cheetahs, however, are an easier mark.

When my son Steven moved to what was then called South-West Africa, he joined my good friend Jan Oelofse on the private game reserve he established. The former German colony, now independent and renamed Namibia, is my favorite land. It has everything an explorer or zoologist dreams about. The sand dunes of the Namib Desert spread along the Atlantic and contain 80 percent of the world's diamonds. To the east is the great Kalahari Desert inhabited by the last of the Bushmen. The north, the highlands, is great animal country. The beautiful Kunene River, with its many waterfalls, forms the border with Angola and equals our Grand Canyon in beauty. South of it is the great Etosha Reserve, known for its elephants, lions, and mirages. The Kaoko Veld, in the northwest, is a most arid, desolate mountain range, penetrated only by brave prospectors, geologists, and zoologists. The mineral wealth of these mountains staggers the mind. Every strategic material, everything needed for armaments and electronics, can be found here, including vanadium, titanium, molybdenum, and the world's greatest uranium deposits. But the land is rough, only the hardy survive, and so the population is one person per square kilometer. Nevertheless, the rarest large antelopes, who require little water, inhabit this territory. They are the greater kudu, which to me is the most beautiful antelope in the world, the Cape oryx with the skeletonlike mask of a witch doctor, the Roberts hartebeest, the mountain zebra, and a few special gazelles, among them the springbok, the steinbok, and the klipspringer, which can jump fifty feet from mountain crag to giant boulder. Giraffes are everywhere.

Only the center highlands are fit for cattle raising and this is where the German colonists had their herds. They soon learned that lions and cattle do not mix, so for their own economic reasons the farmers shot the lions. Thus, the cheetahs, which were no threat to the cattle, had no competition. When we established our game reserve and built the Oelofse House, which is now our home, we learned with great surprise that cheetahs were in greater abundance than anybody wanted. Our purpose was to re-establish near-extinct wildlife, and now the cheetahs preyed on the calves of the mountain zebra, the young of the oryx, and the greater kudu. In our new reserve, the cheetah became a pest.

In the end, the cheetahs had to be trapped or tranquilized from helicopters and moved away. Again I learned how similar animals are to men. I am thinking of the persecuted Russian Jews who fled from the attacks of the Cossacks under the Czar and emigrated to the United States and other countries. The cheetah emigrated, in the same way, to northern Namibia where the "Cossacks" (the lions) could no longer harass them, and here they flourished. Somewhat the same is true of leopards. A few years ago, the World Wildlife Fund took the view that leopards, because they were so widely poached for their beautiful pelts, were an endangered species in Africa. Further exploration, however, proved that they had simply withdrawn into remote and nearly inaccessible forest ranges.

I learned to discount a familiar lie. There is no such thing as a "balance of nature." Nature is never in balance. For fifty years the grass eaters ("grazers") flourish, until they destroy all

Jan Oelofse has a cheetah by the tail

the grass and only trees remain and the forests take over. Then the grass eaters die out or diminish and the quadrupeds who feed on trees and bushes ("browsers") flourish for the next thirty years. By the time all the trees are destroyed, the grass has grown back. The browsers move out or die out, and the grass eaters have their comeback. The same thing happens with climate. The temperature drops a few degrees, and the snow does not melt in the northern hemisphere. The ice caps grow thicker and cool off the earth. Migration to the south begins. Even the continents refuse to stay in the same place. Once Europe, Africa, and the Americas were one big continent and now they have moved thousands of miles apart. But animal life reminds us of how it used to be. The freshwater eels from the Mississippi and from the European rivers still migrate to the same point in the Atlantic, the Sargasso Sea, to lay their eggs. This was the point where the three continents once connected and where eels originated. The genes in the eels still remember where the great granddaddy of all eels was born, and they go "home" year after year through rivers and ocean currents. It is a greater miracle than walking on water. Nature's God manifests miracles a thousand ways.

Another human/animal similarity I have observed on my trips to wild places is that many human tribes refuse to live with neighbors. The aborigines of Australia, the Bushmen of the Kalahari, the Pygmy, the American Indians, all are loners and prefer to be isolated. In the animal world, the cheetah is a solitary creature and moves away from the pressure of other species; the same is true of the leopard. But the lion does not have this genetic tendency, nor does the elephant. Likewise, gorillas and orangutans prefer to avoid neighbors and commotion, while baboons and rhesus monkeys are content in such circumstances.

When I had my camp on the Umfolozi River, every morning I was able to observe the spoors of two leopards going down to the river, but I never could spot the leopards. They were like Greta Garbo in their wanting to be alone. If one understands the animal's needs and desires and respects them, then nature has very little threat for anyone. But many travelers in Africa are very naive about those needs and desires. For instance, a German tourist once wanted to photograph a bull elephant in Kruger Park. Since the elephant's head was not facing the camera, the tourist honked his car horn, not realizing that the hearing of an elephant may be as much as fifty times better than that of a human. The elephant did not at all like the ear-splitting noise and he charged the Volkswagen, picking it up on his two great tusks, carrying it for fifty feet, then dropping it. Then he sat down on the hood. Luckily, his 10,000-pound weight exploded the tires; the elephant mistook the explosion for gunshots and quickly ran away, so the tourist remained unharmed.

I was luckier. I was following elephants in high grass and my cameraman, John Pearson,* was photographing me from his Land-Rover. I looked up as I walked, watching the elephants a few hundred yards ahead of me. As I walked, I accidentally stepped on a leopard sleeping in the very high grass—which gave me a 90 percent chance of being killed instantly. Instead, the leopard took off and disappeared. The topper to this story is that I never saw the leopard I flushed out, though Pearson and his camera saw it. The whole incident occurred so fast that it lasted only half a second on film, and later, to make the scene noticeable to audiences, I had to cheat a little. I found a tame leopard while *Born Free* was being filmed and we took shots of that leopard running through high grass. We then added his run to our true-to-life scene. But

---

* I recently learned that John Pearson was murdered in the Ngorongoro Crater by a game guard. Why and how was not revealed. It was sad news, for he was a good friend of mine as well as a great cameraman; we had worked together for years in Africa. I am sure, however, that John preferred to die in the Ngorongoro Crater—next to the Olduvai Gorge, where human life began—rather than anywhere else in the world. This was the place where I first met him and where I hired him for my *Animal Encyclopedia*. He loved living in Africa more than life itself.

after that close call I watched my step very carefully while walking in high grass.

I mentioned previously that cheetahs are the fastest mammals. In 1963 I conducted a number of experiments to clock the speed of African animals by chasing them in flat terrain with my new Land-Rover. I could not keep up with the cheetah at fifty-five miles per hour; the gazelles and ostriches ran close to fifty miles an hour. The cheetah, which feeds on both gazelles and ostriches, naturally must top the speed of the prey in order to catch up with them. Again, by natural selection, only those cheetahs that could run faster than fast gazelles have survived. Checking Guinness's mammalian speed table in *Animal Facts and Feats,* you will find that cheetahs are clocked at sixty-three miles per hour. This is not as amazing to me as a 10,000-pound elephant running at twenty-five miles per hour, or a rhino at an even faster twenty-eight miles per hour.

Because of the cheetah's natural disposition to chase and kill fast-running antelopes, Oriental princes used them on their hunts for thousands of years; in fact, another name for cheetah was hunting leopard. Captured as cubs, the cheetahs were tamed, treated well, and taken on hunts in chariots of royalty. The cheetah wore a black mask over its eyes, and when a deer or an antelope appeared, the mask was removed. The cheetah would spot the deer, chase it down, and kill it for the prince. It then returned to the chariot where it was rewarded with a ladleful of the finest animal fat, which was the cheetah's favorite delicacy and bribe. The cheetah is nearly nonexistent now in the Orient, as are the royal princes in most of the East. The African princes treated cheetahs rather worse, as shown by the fact that almost every black tribal chief or dignitary wears the spotted fur of a cheetah to signify importance. It's no wonder that East Africa has so few cheetahs.

Another elegant, beautiful cat of the African wild and a na-

Ivan Tors and a leopard, face to face (*Photo by John Pearson*)

tive of Asia is the leopard. Hunted for their pelts, leopards became extremely shy of men in the past century.

In South-West Africa, while catching wild game, my son Steve has spotted leopard spoors frequently but without seeing a leopard. I was on six African expeditions before I saw my first leopard. The shyness of the leopard is a lucky thing for us humans because the leopard and his South American relative, the jaguar, are the strongest of all predators, pound for pound. They are better killers than any other creatures. Their fangs and claws can tear apart in a few seconds anything that weighs under three hundred pounds. It is lucky that they usually kill only when they are hungry.

Leopards are so fast that they are nearly invisible. When we photographed the killing of a big impala buck by two leopards, the action went by so quickly that, in doing the film, we had to repeat every frame six times, making the scene six times longer than the real action so that their mode of attack could be observed. A mother and a nearly full grown leopard had attacked a male impala. One jumped on his neck, breaking it, and the other attached herself to the impala's muzzle, suffocating it just in case the broken neck did not suffice.

My son David was present at this kill and I was very worried at first that the experience might be traumatic for a nine-year-old boy, but I was wrong. The attack of the leopards was so fast, so graceful, and death came so quickly to the impala that for the first time I felt that killing can be a graceful thing. David was not bothered at all.

Soon after, we found the impala draped over the fork of a tree. Leopards, with their amazing strength, can climb a tree vertically, with a burden twice their own weight, to hang the carcass where it is safe from vultures, lions, jackals, and hyenas. Leopards do not enjoy fresh meat. They chew on the carcass for many days and like it best when it is rotten. For this reason their bite can be very infectious to a human. Until the advent of antibiotics, leopard bites resulted in amputation or death.

My son Peter trained a leopard for a film in Africa. The leopard was supposed to attack him and bite into his shirt sleeve. The leopard learned this quickly but my son made a big mistake. One morning he put on a T-shirt. He did not plan to exercise the leopard, but the leopard was not informed of this. When he saw Peter he jumped on him, trying to bite into his shirt sleeve which, of course, was not there. He bit into the T-shirt and through my son's right biceps. As he was not vicious, he did not tear the flesh but punched two big holes in the muscle. My son was driven to a hospital where he was treated with a tetanus shot and penicillin. Still, by nightfall his arm was infected and swollen. Lab tests had to be made to determine which antibiotic would kill the infection. Luckily, one out of five proved effective and my son's wound healed in a few days. Thirty years ago such a bite would have cost him his arm.

Both cheetahs and leopards are loners who hide from humans. During the day, they usually stay in trees, in the shade of high branches, blending into the surroundings; or they may rest in caves, where it is cool. They mate by picking up the scent of a female in heat, and their great olfactory senses will point toward a female even if she is thirty miles away. I recall an incident that happened near Nairobi. Two Europeans, living many miles apart, had tame cheetahs tied up in their back yards. One had a male, the other a female. Neither of the owners knew about the other. When the female came in heat, the male broke his leash, jumped over the fence, and made his way through a forest, over a mountain, and through the city of Nairobi itself, a real metropolis with bumper-to-bumper traffic, and reached the female.

In the world of cheetahs, the female is left alone after the mating and she is responsible for hunting and child care. But the leopards are less male chauvinist. After mating, they stay with the female through birth and hunt for the family for a few months. The leopard's strength, according to a scale established by Ralph Helfer (my partner at Africa USA), is five to one: one pound of leopard muscle equals five pounds of human muscle. A hundred-pound leopard has the muscle strength of three strong men, making him proportionally stronger than a lion or tiger.

I had an unusual experience with a leopard in Miami while shooting my television series *Flipper*. One day I received a call from a young lady I did not know. With the innocent voice of a Marilyn Monroe, she told me her trouble. She was a model and she lived in a fancy apartment on Miami Beach. The year before, she had received, as a Christmas present from an admirer in Kenya, a baby leopard. She loved the cub. He slept in her bed and ate whatever she ate, including bacon and eggs for breakfast. But when the neighbors found out about the leopard, they reported it to the police. She was served with a court order to get rid of the leopard, and so she had called me, saying she would trust no one but me with his well being. Would I buy him or take him from her? I drove over to her home, and when I entered the elegant apartment I found a beautiful young blonde in a lace negligee, with a full-grown male leopard at her feet. The leopard did not seem to mind my presence. I rubbed his fur, scratched his ears, and without any problems he accepted me as a friend.

As the young lady and I discussed arrangements for the leopard, there was a knock on the door. I opened the door and there stood the chief of detectives, a dark Italian-looking gentleman, who wanted to be sure that the leopard was out of the apartment. When the leopard saw him, he leaped. I shut the door in the detective's face, thus saving his life. When the leopard had settled down, I cautiously left the room. The detective stood outside with a gun in his hand, ready to shoot the leopard. I, myself, was not quite sure why the leopard had reacted so savagely. Did he know the detective's intention? Or was he actually a dangerous beast? Anyhow, I assured the detective that I accepted full responsibility and that the leopard would be caged and air-freighted immediately to my animal compound in California.

I paid the young lady five hundred dollars and shipped the leopard to Africa USA. I placed him in an airy, extra large cage made of aluminum, out of which the leopard could see from any angle. He was so happy to see me that when I entered the cage he leaped around me, licking my hand and my face. I could play with him as I could with any of our pet animals, but when one of my trainers with black hair entered the cage, the leopard bit a chunk out of his buttock. Ralph Helfer's wife, an ash-blond beauty, was accepted by the beast at once, as was my wife who was also a blonde. My gray hair and white beard were acceptable to the leopard as blond, but otherwise, all through his life he was gentle with blondes only. After all, the blond model had been his surrogate mother, and so the leopard trusted only people who looked like her.

The Miami leopard is a classic example of animal imprinting. When a baby duck hatches, if the first thing she sees is not her mother but a turtle, she will follow the turtle. And so it is with most wildlife. This is the way we brought up our animal babies. In Africa USA, we tried to imprint all our newborn with the image of our trainers. Our best female trainer, Pat Derby, at one time had a Himalayan sun bear and a baby elephant to take care of. The sibling rivalry was enormous. Whenever she picked up the bear cub, the 300-pound baby elephant ran to her and wanted to be picked up too. As Pat weighed less than a hundred pounds, she could not quite handle it.

Leopards and lions have not changed for millions of years, proof they have evolved to perfection. Their survival, I believe, is more assured than human survival is. We may not see many leopards because their hiding places are so remote, but they are there. We read their spoors. They stalk invisibly, they kill fast, hide their kills, and come out only when they think it is safe. But leopards have one weakness. To them, dogs are a delicacy, and no dog is safe in leopard country. It has happened again and again that normally shy leopards have jumped through open windows, entered rooms, and picked off dogs from inside a house or from porches or gardens, and carried them away. But luckily they also love baboons, and the hills where leopards live are full of baboons. This is the reason that leopards do not endanger our wildlife breeding program on the Oelofse farm. Still, during the night we lock our dogs in kennels.

In Magadi, Kenya, I have a friend who built a modern house with a big glass window overlooking the magnificent Great Rift Valley. One night he was reading a book in his favorite arm chair, with his dog at his feet. Suddenly, he looked up to see a leopard jumping against the window, trying to get to his dog. Luckily the window was strong enough that the leopard only banged his head and then galloped away in pain. Next day when someone visited my friend, he told the story and tapped the glass, pointing out the spot where the leopard hit. As he touched it, the glass wall shattered into a thousand pieces. Suddenly he realized that the leopard, by exerting only a bit more force, could have been in his living room, to kill him and carry away his dog. He immediately redesigned the window and equipped it with bars, giving up most of his great view.

A leopard may be shy in general but he is never stupid, and he learns quickly from experience. My friend Reggie Destro, one of the finest African hunting guides, always took his clients to the same place in Tanzania for buffalo hunts. He had found out a long time ago that buffaloes in this remote sector were the best trophies, so he never hunted anything there but buffalo. After each hunt, the native bearers sawed off the horns and left the meat because it was too heavy a bulk to cart away. The local leopard soon learned that after a buffalo hunt there would be a free lunch, and he could hardly wait in his hide-out to hear a shot telling him that a buffalo had been killed. He became so impatient that he usually appeared long before the safari company had left. After a few years, Reggie had only to shoot off his gun and the leopard would immediately appear in the open, waiting for a buffalo to be killed. Then after everyone left, he nonchalantly started his meal. This is a good example of what is called "operant conditioning" in psychology.

We use this method when we work with animals in films. One of our trainers stands with a chunk of meat and a buzzer. We set up the camera at one end of the set, and place the caged animal in a strategic position at the other end. The camera starts to roll. The trainer sounds the buzzer. The cage door opens. The leopard, lion, tiger, or wolf knows from the buzz that it is feeding time. So he runs straight to the trainer for a chunk of meat. When we place actors in the background, the animal runs in front of our actors, and this appears to the camera eye as if the actors are in great danger as the beast charges. When he has eaten the meat, we place another chunk in his cage and sound the buzzer there. The animal rushes back to his cage to finish his lunch and we get another shot of the beast and the actors together.

Today, in African game reserves, very few animals are shy of people. They have learned about Land-Rovers and tourist

Ivan Tors and one of his actors read a movie script
(*Metro-Goldwyn-Mayer*)

buses, and they are aware that here they are safe from men. That is why one can see more leopards, more lions, more cheetahs at a reserve than in truly wild country. All they have to fear here is each other because they are not fed, and thus the predator must kill his prey. I am not fond of some of the game reserves — places where the number of tourists is not controlled, places where the lions are surrounded by cars and buses and tourists snapping photos. Also, the car wheels erode the grassland, and air quality is endangered by the dust these vehicles whip up. Somehow, I find the whole setting obscene. The creatures have no privacy, not even at their water hole or when they copulate. I wish we could have another solution, such as making tourists invisible with invisible paint.

3   My Friends the Elephants

THERE WAS DENSE BRUSH between the dirt road and the dried out riverbed. We stopped our Volkswagen van as we heard the crackling of twigs. It was the distinctive sound of foraging elephants. We opened the sun roof and climbed on top. The gray backs of about twenty-five elephants were visible above the brushline. We could spot a tiny water hole in the dried out riverbed. In a perfect demonstration of motherly love, a giant female with her nimble trunk sucked up some water, then showered her overheated baby. Sven Persson, my fearless Swedish cameraman, prepared his noiseless Arriflex camera and sneaked into the bushes, signaling me to stay put. Two men make more noise than one, and to get an exceptional shot of mother and baby from a closer angle was all-important.

Sven was a perfectionist, so I was prepared to wait for him for many hours. I reclined on the center seat of the van. I opened the sun roof and all the doors and windows to allow more ventilation in the ninety-degree tropical heat. I soon dozed off. Suddenly I awakened. A giant shadow loomed over my head. I looked up without moving. Above me, I could distinguish the tiny eyes of a bull elephant. The slits of the musth glands were wet between the eyes and the ears. The bull was a giant. His great ivory tusks would have been worth thousands of dollars to a hunter. He was absolutely silent, just as I was.

He moved his six-foot long agile trunk along my body, examining every inch of me. Any move on my part could startle this bull. My only salvation was to lie there as though paralyzed. The human scent intrigued him, but as long as I was motionless, I was fairly safe. He studied me for about two minutes. Then he lifted his great head, pulled his trunk up, and moved away from the van, walking down the road, rejoining the herd.

I shut the door and the sun roof. Then Sven reappeared from the bushes. A happy smile on his sunburned face told me that he had got the shot — a mother elephant showering her baby. He climbed in and motioned to me to drive on. When we reached a curve, the elephant herd was about to cross the road fifty yards ahead of our car. The female sentry noticed us, abruptly stopped. The entire long line of elephant females and babies stopped in unison, as though they had been connected by an invisible umbilical cord. The sentry elephant looked at us and waited for a command from the matriarch, the largest of the females, who was still somewhere in the brush. Then she must have received the signal, "It's O.K., you can cross."

Sven opened the sun roof and photographed the long line of elephants crossing the road. In the center walked the great she-elephant, the absolute, benevolent ruler of this highly civilized herd. Then another giant female, a guard, suddenly charged us. I had kept the engine running and I now put the car in reverse and backed away another fifty yards. The charging elephant stopped. Soon I understood the unexpected hostility. A group of young elephant babies was about to cross the road and the herd was worried about their safety. The guard kept threatening us, relaying the message to keep our distance. When the babies were safely in the dense brush on the other side of the road, the guard elephant rejoined the column. But the last elephant, an old giant with one tusk who was another sentry, stayed on the road until she knew that the herd was safe from any human threat. Then she, too, moved on, giving us the right of way. By the time we passed the place of crossing, the gray ghosts had disappeared into the brush.

I consider the society of elephants the most civilized land-mammal organization on earth, including the human one. Elephants are the biggest, the strongest of all land creatures, but they use their power for protection, rarely for aggression.

My first encounter with a herd of elephants occurred many, many years ago on the slopes of Kilimanjaro. We had surprised a herd of sixty-two elephants with our jeep when we were about forty yards from the leader. We stopped the jeep but kept the engine running. I could see clearly that the matriarch and her lady adjutant were holding a palaver, their trunks touching each other. The conversation between them must have gone something like this: "You keep charging the jeep, while I lead the rest around the mound and meet you nine miles from here at Lake Marangu."

The next thing that happened was that the big female extended her giant ears, whipped her trunk around, shook her giant head menacingly, then charged the jeep. My companion,

Ivan Tors meets some new arrivals at Africa USA (*Metro-Goldwyn-Mayer*)

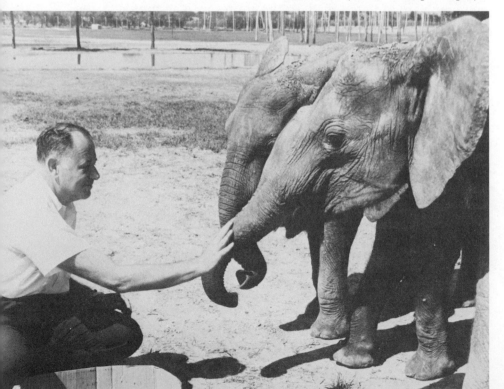

an old African hand, said, "Don't move. She's bluffing." He was right. The elephant stopped ten yards short of our car, scaring the daylights out of me but not my companion, who knew elephants. The big female kept threatening us until the rest of the herd had disappeared safely behind the mountain. Then she, too, ambled away, but in the opposite direction. She knew that if she rejoined the herd now, she would give away the location of her family. So she circled the mountain, counterclockwise, while the herd moved around the hill clockwise. My companion, Colonel Scott, wanted to demonstrate to me how smart elephants were, so we drove about five hundred feet higher. We got out of the jeep and climbed onto the top of a rock. From there I could see the herd and the sentry on the slope through my binoculars, as they came from opposite directions to meet at the rendezvous point. Since that day, my admiration for elephants has been infinite.

The birth of a baby elephant is an incredible sight. While I have observed baby elephants just a few hours after they were born, I have friends who have witnessed the actual birth. Before birth, the pregnant mother leaves the herd with her best female friend, who will act as the nanny. The two of them clear an area in the brush or forest, which will function as the delivery room. They stamp their giant feet, pulverizing everything in the clearing, leaving the ground covered only with dust. The gestation period for a baby elephant is between twenty-two and twenty-four months. The newborn weighs between two hundred and three hundred pounds and actually falls out, still in the giant placenta, by the pull of gravity. The umbilical cord snaps as the calf is born. When the placenta breaks and the baby is freed, mother and midwife lovingly clean the baby. The two female elephants, aware that the amniotic fluid has a strong odor that may attract predators, work quickly to get rid of the afterbirth by plowing all this material underground, and then they clean the baby with a shower of sand. The sand is used here as baby powder.

A newborn elephant is completely viable. The baby looks exactly like a miniature adult and will stand up without much difficulty, although the trunks of the two females will support the newborn. The smell of the milk will attract the infant to the mother's udders, which are between the forelegs, unlike those of other ungulates such as cattle and antelopes.

The nanny will guard mother and child while the mother is feeding her young. I have followed them to the water hole where mother teaches the young one how to suck water into its tiny trunk, then squirt the water into its mouth, which is the way all elephants drink. The young elephants take to water with great joy. Both mother and nanny are extremely careful. If the baby slips in the mud, two trunks reach under the baby's chest and lift it to its feet. I found this quite miraculous since the baby was not within the adults' field of vision. Still, the two females always seem to know where the baby is and when it needs their support. The baby elephant will stay in the close vicinity of the mother for many years and learn the ways of the elephant by imitation.

The perfect place to observe elephants is at a water hole, for elephants consume a great deal of water and must drink at least every second day to survive. An adult elephant will drink between forty and eighty gallons of water. If the water holes go dry, the elephants die. However, the elephant is the only creature besides man that can dig a water hole. I have witnessed such a feat in the dried out Letaba River. The elephants wandered into the middle of the riverbed, and the strongest bulls and the largest females began to dig with their tusks and forefeet where they smelled water below. In half an hour, they had dug a four-foot-deep hole. They then inserted their trunks, and by sucking they created a vacuum that sipped up water from below. The water began to flow into their trunks through the soft sand. A new well had been created. We once photographed a whole sector full of elephant-made wells, which had saved not only the elephants but all the other animals in the region, who did not possess the intellect and the strength of an elephant.

Our most interesting encounter with elephants took place on a day that began with my arrival at the Palabora airstrip, where Sven was waiting for me. We got into the four-wheel-drive truck with our twenty-five rolls of film and headed for elephant country. It was a hot and dry year. There was very little water in the rivers and only the best water holes contained any water at all. We stopped at a well-known water hole and looked for elephant spoors. There were none. "There have been no elephants here for at least a week," said Sven disappointedly. Then I looked to my left and saw about sixty elephants coming in our direction. I looked to my right, and I spotted another herd coming toward us. I looked up and saw a huge tree. In no time at all, Sven and I had hidden our car in a ditch and were perched on top of the tree with our cameras, film, and some oranges to quench our thirst in the hundred-degree dry heat, in the event that we had to stay up there for more than a few hours.

Sven and I roosted on top of the tree for nine long hours. Our bodies were aching but there was no way to get down while the elephants were under us. The oranges probably saved us from dehydration and I learned more about elephants in one day than I would have in four years in a classroom.

As soon as the first herd arrived, the elephants posted a sentry at our tree. They knew very well that we were there because they had probably picked up our scent a mile away, but the elephants were thirsty and, since they did not smell gunpowder or firearms, they thought we did not present a great threat. But to make sure, a large tusker took up position right under us, resting her trunk on a limb to pick up any movement we might dare to make. The rest of the herd moved to the water hole in a deliberate, civilized manner, giving way to each other, no one pushing, no one trying to be the first.

Elephants step into the water and go through a ritual before drinking. If their bodies are too hot, swallowing gallons of cool water may be a shock to the system. So, before they start to drink, they splash water with their agile trunks over their giant earlobes. The ears are crisscrossed by blood vessels. As the blood vessels cool off, so does the body. The body heat thus reduced, the elephants begin to drink earnestly. Their thirst quenched, they lie down in the pool to cool and clean their entire bodies. The young elephants splash and play, shake their tiny trunks merrily, never leaving the proximity of mother and nanny. What always amazes me is how the young often stays under the belly of its mother so as to be shaded from the hot sun, and neither the mother nor the nanny ever steps on a baby, or even bumps him — as though they have eyes or sonar or radar in every part of their magnificent bodies.

Actually, the elephants' most important sensory organ is the trunk, with its millions of olfactory receptors. Elephants can, in a manner of speaking, read with their noses. When an elephant rejoins the herd, the others can tell by the scent molecules on its body where that elephant has been, what kind of trees it has passed, whether it was near water, and whether it has met other elephants. All of these bits of information are inscribed in scent on the newcomer's hide.

Ivan Tors elephant watching in East Africa

But our most important observation that day was of the highly civilized interaction between the two herds at the water hole. The first herd arrived. They spent only a half hour in the water and then gave way to the other herd. Normally they would spend many hours in the pool, but today they respected the rights of others. The second herd was just as civilized as the first one. In about an hour, the number-two herd moved out of the water and allowed the first herd to return and refresh themselves again.

Relieved of thirst, they withdrew to the shade. Then they showered themselves with sand, which serves two important purposes. The first is cooling, the other is caking. The sand cakes quickly on the wet bodies and traps the parasites, ticks, and flies. As the mud dries, the elephants rub their bodies against trees and logs and the trapped insects fall off.

In the meantime, we could observe love play among the young adults as they caressed each other and examined each other with their trunks. Often, they would kiss each other. Mothers touched their young. My overall feeling while observing a herd was pleasure in the way these gray giants care for each other, protect and respect each other. They seem to be both full of feeling and socially very well organized.

We, however, at the top of our big tree, were feeling in real trouble. It was blazing hot and the elephants refused to move from the water hole. If we climbed down, we'd be among them. The sentry was now asleep, but her trunk was still resting on our tree. Our bodies ached. Our thirst was enormous. Our water was in the truck and there was no way to get to it. And the bulls had not yet arrived.

In my forty trips to Africa, I have met with very few herds that combined adult bulls and their females. A normal herd consists of females and male subadults. The oldest female acts as the matriarch; and most of the other members of the herd are her sisters, children, and grandchildren. Bulls are tolerated until they reach the mating age only; then they join the older bulls. The bulls keep close by but do not mix with the herd.

Only the strongest bull is allowed to mate. He joins the herd when a female is in heat and ready to be covered. Otherwise, the bulls form a bachelor party and stick together.

To our chagrin, the bulls arrived at the water hole directly after the two herds had finished watering and had moved on. Now there were three giant bulls lounging around the water hole. Our buttocks could no longer stand the pain caused by our uncomfortable perch. My muscles ached all over, and I told Sven that, no matter what, I must get down. Our female sentry had departed with the herd, so Sven and I descended from the tree, carrying equipment and film, and passed behind the bulls at a distance of about fifteen feet. To our pleasant surprise, the big bulls couldn't have cared less about us. We posed no threat to them now that the babies were gone. They did not even sniff at us. To them, we were just oversized baboons. We reached our truck and drove safely away. The result of the day was five hours of film on elephant group behavior and their care for the young — and aching bones. I consider it one of the most interesting and productive days of my life.

In the past, books about elephants described the bull as a dangerous animal, always attacking the hunter. This may be true, since most hunters go after the big tuskers. But not being a hunter, I must state that I have never been bothered by a bull. In fact, it was a bull that showed me that elephants have a sense of humor. Once, Sven and I were hiding behind a giant log, trying to photograph three big bulls as they were passing by. As they reached us, they stopped. The tips of their trunks turned toward us like radar, picking up our scent. The lead bull now knew that we were hiding behind the giant tree trunk. He did not want to harm us, but he wanted to show us that we weren't fooling him, so he gingerly picked up a twig and skillfully flipped it over the log, right onto Sven's head. Then, looking very satisfied, he moved on. Sven got this incident on film.

In my experience, the only danger from elephants comes from their great maternal instinct, which is their virtue. I must admit that I have had a few close calls. One was on the bank of the Mara River, in Masai territory. An elephant herd passed by my Land-Rover and disappeared into the riverine forest. I got out of the Land-Rover and looked down the steep bank, admiring about twelve basking crocodiles. Suddenly, coming from the bushes to my right, I heard the fearful trumpeting of a baby elephant. By some unusual mistake, or perhaps they were scared by my vehicle, the departing herd had left the baby behind. The baby's call for help made the herd turn around and stampede through the grass in my direction. I saw thirty elephants, weighing at least four tons each, galloping toward me. I had only one route of escape — into the river among the twelve huge crocodiles. Having no choice, I jumped. My splash in the water scared the daylights out of the crocodiles. They scattered faster than I could scamper for the far bank. Climbing out of the Mara, I was less afraid of the crocodiles than of the elephants. This is how I learned to appreciate crocodiles.

Another time, we were landing in a helicopter when we noticed a female elephant with a sick baby. We decided to tranquilize the mother and to treat the baby. But before we could get our hypodermic gun out, the mother charged the chopper. The rotating blades could have cut her up, but she did not care. Her baby was threatened and she was ready to take on the machine, to destroy herself and us, in the attempt to save her offspring. Luckily we were able to take off before the elephant reached the chopper. Then my friend Jan Oelofse, with his finest marksmanship, shot a hypodermic dart into the buttock of the mother from an altitude of fifty feet. The great lady staggered for a while, then lay down to sleep.

We landed and tried to catch the baby. As I was the first one out, I jumped on him, but I had no idea how strong a baby elephant could be. As he darted away from me, I grabbed his tail. The tiny elephant pulled me through the bushes with the greatest of ease. I weigh two hundred pounds, but the baby weighed around two hundred fifty. I became a living toboggan as I skidded through the underbrush. But finally, five of us overpowered the squealing, trumpeting calf. He had very bad sores in the genital area, and we treated him with antibiotics and ointments while we wrestled with him for dear life—our dear life. When we had completed the treatment, Oelofse gave the mother elephant an antidote. Baby joined the sleeping mother and we took off in our chopper. From above we observed the reunion of the awakened, though slightly hung over, mother and the medicated baby that had given such a rough time to five big strong males of the puny human race.

The solidarity of elephants is legendary. I witnessed the following incident near the Letaba River in Kruger National Park. The tourist camp is surrounded by a strong fence to keep the elephants out, but the fruit trees were blooming, giving off a scent irresistible to an elephant. So, every night an old bull elephant tore down a section of the fence and entered the park to feed on the fruit trees. His younger bachelor companion did not have the courage of the old bull, so he never joined him on these nightly excursions. The game warden became annoyed by the daily task of repairing the fence, and besides, he was worried about the safety of the tourists. So one day, he tracked down the guilty bull and shot him. His assistant sawed off the giant tusks and carried them into the camp and laid them on the porch to dry. The next night, the old bull's companion tore down the fence, walked to the house, picked up the tusks with his trunk, and carried them away. I was told that the young bull was seen for days carrying the tusks of his friend. No one knows where he buried them.

There is a lot of controversy about the sleeping habits of elephants. Elephants are night creatures. They feed in the dark, when it is cooler, and a herd may move thirty miles in one night while feeding. It is very seldom that an elephant can be seen asleep. In my whole life, I have seen only two elephants asleep. One was asleep lying down and snorting like a locomotive. The other elephant was asleep standing up. When they are asleep standing, they are more dangerous, as it is easier to startle them, and a startled elephant may turn into a furious elephant. We were staying at Governor's Camp on the Mara River, filming my *Encyclopedia of Wildlife,* when our British cameraman, John Pearson, awoke in his tent. He looked at his watch. It was 6:00 A.M. He stepped out of his tent and, to his great surprise, there was a 10,000-pound elephant standing next to his tent, snoring. John suddenly realized that 6:00 A.M. was the time when the house boy usually brought the morning tea to all the guests in the tents. Just then, the boy arrived with a large tray full of china teacups. Seeing the elephant, the boy dropped the tray and started to run away. The teacups clattered loudly as they hit the ground, awakening the elephant. Startled, the elephant broke into a run; but his feet tangled in the guide ropes of the tents, pulling most of them down, and he dragged them along behind him. Luckily no one got hurt, and the elephant, having had his scare, never came back to our camp again. After all, elephants never forget!

Even this platitude has some merit. While making *Daktari,* we had about nine elephants on our California animal ranch. My favorite was Margie, a seven-year-old. Margie loved mints. Whenever I went to the ranch, I would put a mint in my mouth. Margie knew this and she would immediately come to me and extend her trunk. I would take the tip of her trunk in my hand and blow the mint into her trunk. Margie loved this.

After the ranch buildings were destroyed in 1968 by a sudden, violent flood I did not rebuild. Instead, I sold the animals, including Margie, and left for Africa. Six years later I returned to the United States to film a zoological special for German television, and, while searching for locations, I found myself in an animal park close to San Francisco. As I walked along the road, a big female elephant appeared with her keeper a few feet behind her. Suddenly the elephant rushed up to me and extended her trunk the way Margie used to do. I knew it was Margie. Luckily I had mints with me, and when I blew them into her trunk, the reunion was complete. Six years had passed and Margie had not forgotten me. My appearance had

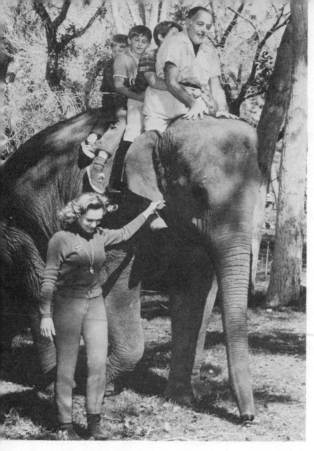

Mrs. Tors leads Margie with (left to right) David, 5; Peter, 10; Steven, 11; and Ivan Tors aboard

changed, her appearance had changed, but elephants are very special creatures.

I tried the mint trick once more. I arrived in Bangkok one morning and a TWA car drove me from the airport to the newly opened Dusit Thani Hotel, a deluxe establishment. The doorman was dressed like Yul Brynner in *The King and I,* and next to him stood a young, tame Indian elephant. I was chewing on a mint as I stepped out of the car. When I saw the elephant, I blew the mint flavor into her trunk. It was like magic! The little elephant walked alongside me as I went into the lobby and she was at my side while I checked in. The people in the hotel stared at us in amazement, laughed and clapped their hands in delight. But getting into the elevator was a no-no! The doorman and the bellboys had to use force to keep the elephant away from me as I stepped into the elevator. The Dusit

Thani elephant and I remained buddies throughout my stay in Bangkok.

In Ceylon (now Sri Lanka) and India, I studied the relationship between working elephants and their keepers, the mahouts, who remain with the same elephant until the elephant dies. This elephant/human relationship is extraordinary. Of course, the elephant is a very valuable possession — being truck, bulldozer, plow, and road builder — so the mahout takes care of his elephant with devotion. He won't let the elephant work when the sun is high; he will lead it to a river or lake, where he scrubs him, rubs him, and babies his big body. The mahout's oldest son is usually with him, and when the mahout dies, the son inherits the job. The elephants are equally grateful and obedient. The elephant's wisdom is shown again when he picks up heavy timber. He looks for perfect balance. He judges the center of gravity before lifting the log in his curled trunk, so that each side will weigh about the same. What I observed there was a close and gentle relationship between the 4-ton beasts and their 120-pound caretakers.

The loveliest scene I ever witnessed took place in Soledad Canyon, California. One of our elephants was missing from Africa USA. She had broken her tether and had disappeared. We searched and searched in the surrounding woods but could not find her spoor. Finally, we received a telephone call from one of the neighbors, about two miles away, telling us that an elephant was in the backyard. When we got there, we saw an incredible sight! Our elephant and a little girl were seesawing together! The elephant had her foreleg on one side and the little girl was straddled on the other end of the seesaw. The little girl was absolutely unafraid of the elephant. In fact, she screamed when we took "her" elephant away.

No wonder that the natives have such respect for elephants. The Queen Mother in Swaziland is still called the She Elephant, meaning "possessed of wisdom, loyalty, love and protective care."

4   My African Sons

STEVEN, PETER, AND DAVID were born in California, and now all of them live in southern Africa. They were introduced to that land in 1970 — shortly after my wife, Constance, died — when I had an assignment from NBC to make a film about the African elephants. David was nine; Pete, thirteen; and Steve, fourteen. At that time, a mansion in Beverly Hills was our home. There were five servants in the house and the boys were driven to school each day by a chauffeur. Everyone, in fact, seemed ready to spoil them. So the boys' first African experience, beginning with our arrival in Nairobi, had a profound effect on all of them.

My first phone call was to my good friend Dr. Leakey, the world-famous anthropologist. He said, "Come right over. I've lots to show you." The boys had learned about Leakey in school and from my stories, and they were impressed to be meeting this Einstein of anthropology. They had their first culture shock when we arrived at the Leakey home. The modest house with its rustic wooden furniture, no carpets or couches, was an astonishing change from the omnipresent mansions of Beverly Hills. And Dr. Leakey, the renowned man himself, was a kind, unpretentious old gentleman.

We sat down on a bench and he showed us, with his inexpensive slide projector, the most interesting pictures we had ever seen. His disciple, Dian Fossey, had sent them to him from the Virunga volcano. The pictures depicted her life among a family of gorillas — how she approached them and their reactions to her. I think it took four years before she succeeded in touching her first gorilla. All of it was very exciting. But my children were particularly delighted by the lovely little hyraxes that scampered throughout the Leakey house. The hyrax is a soft, tiny, cuddly, curious, furry creature whose claim to fame is that it is related to the elephant. The skeletal formations of the two are quite similar.

When we took our leave, Dr. Leakey wrote a note to his wife, Mary Leakey, who was in charge of the excavations at the Olduvai Gorge, asking that she show my sons her findings of prehistoric men and animals. I think that night at Dr. Leakey's was a turning point in my children's lives. The boys realized that the Beverly Hills luxury they were used to was not an important part of life. Dr. Leakey was. The little hyraxes were. And a girl living among gorillas was.

They could hardly wait for the next day to see more of Africa. We chartered a plane to Seronara, which is the main camp on the Serengeti Plain, where millions of animals roam. The pilot allowed my boys to take turns copiloting the plane and taught them how to handle the controls. It was a new thrill. Crossing the border between Kenya and Tanzania, we flew over an active volcano, and young David took an incredible photograph that captured the deep interior of the crater.

When we landed on the grass strip in Seronara, we had to be very careful, for the airstrip was full of gazelles. David decided to catch himself a gazelle, which, as we described earlier, is one of the fastest animals. He chased the gazelles for at least twenty minutes, and when he returned empty-handed, he blamed his failure on the fact that he was not wearing his "fast" shoes. We then proceeded to the customs shack to check in. There was a sign on the door: I AM ON SAFARI. We found the official stamp on the desk, stamped our passports, wrote our names and the number of our plane in a register, and took off again to Lake Nadutu, where I was to meet my cameraman, John Pearson, and his wife, Jennie.

In the lodge, we met not only the Pearsons but Jane Goodall and her husband and young son. In the evening, she projected the films of her life with chimpanzees, for which she has become world famous.

My sons learned about Africa fast. The first afternoon, we watched Cape hunting dogs killing their prey and feeding their young. We met lions who ignored us. From our open Land-Rover we spotted a single old hyena and Pearson played hyena sounds on a tape recorder. The hyena, a half mile away, started to come in the direction of the sound. He circled our Land-Rover again and again, looking for the origin of the hyena voices. Finally he accepted the idea that he was hallucinating and moved on. The boys laughed their heads off.

Next morning we drove over to the Olduvai Gorge, where Dr. and Mrs. Leakey had found the first proof of the missing link between apes and men. There, we had a chance to study the completely preserved skeleton of a giant hippo who had lived about 500,000 years ago. This find has shown that the body of the hippo has remained unchanged over the past fifty milleniums — which seems to prove that hippos are perfectly adapted to their surroundings.

From the Olduvai Gorge, we drove to the Ngorongoro Crater with John Pearson. The old crater and the lake, which is the only source of water for more than twenty thousand animals, are among the great wonders of Africa. We saw elephants and rhinos; and lions feeding on zebra. As we ate our box lunches in the shade of a huge umbrella tree, we saw gazelles, elands, giraffes — even a mirage over the lake. It was an enthralling experience for my sons. They felt happier and freer than ever before. They had spent only two days in Africa, but they had already come under its spell. The African mystique had enveloped them and nothing else was any longer satisfying. I became hooked in 1962; they, in 1970; and now it was a family addiction.

To be in love with Africa can be a hazardous romance. The future is uncertain, and there are dangers. But the excitement of living close to nature is indescribable. Watching a cheetah, a herd of elephants, a prehistoric rhino, is like being in an imaginary world. The color, beauty, and clean air raise one to an exalted state of awareness without the aid of drugs. Nothing there has changed intrinsically in six thousand years; everything is basic — the eerie volcanoes of the great Rift Valley, the shimmering heat and sandstorms of the desert, the mirages of the Etosha Pan, the nomads marching with their camels, single file, silhouetted against the rising sun . . . Once Africa has grabbed you, you are captive for life.

When I returned to the States with my sons after our trip, Steven, the eldest, felt particularly restless and out of place in Los Angeles. Already as a child he had shown himself to be unusual. When he was nine years old, he was attacked by a Saint Bernard and was nearly killed. He had twenty-seven severe

A kudu, one of the most elegant African antelopes. This one is so tame that he walks into the house in Namibia in search of books or film to eat.

lacerations on his body, from his chest to his feet. It took 127 sutures to sew him together, an operation performed without anesthetic because the doctors were checking for possible nerve damage. The dog's teeth had scraped the bone on Steve's right arm and he developed a bone infection. He needed painful operations and he nearly lost his arm. It was a terrible trauma for us, the parents, and a great trauma for him. But his reaction was extraordinary. After this near-tragic encounter, he decided that he wanted to know everything about dogs. He bought numerous books about dogs and by the age of ten he was an expert, virtually a walking dog-encyclopedia. He was familiar with every breed, their evolution and anatomy. The incident left no serious aftereffect, and he soon lost his fear of dogs completely. He instinctively knew how to deal with a difficult situation.

Another uncommon side to Steve's character became apparent during that first Africa trip. One day I took him with me to do some filming in the bush. Without warning, we found ourselves surrounded by a herd of wild elephants. It was really scary. He stood next to me as the elephants passed us at very close range. I whispered to him, telling him to freeze. He whispered back to me that he was scared to death. I couldn't blame him, for, at that moment, a giant bull elephant pushed over a huge tree, which made a terrifying crushing noise. Steve was trembling as I held his hands in mine. Later, back in Los Angeles, I was amazed at how he described this incident to his friends, always stressing how scared he had been. I admired him for this. He was free of prideful inhibitions. I, myself, could never have told anyone that I had been frightened; I would have been ashamed of that self-image; to me it would have seemed unmanly. But he knew better than anybody how to overcome his fears.

Three years later, Steve became an elephant tracker in Kenya (a job usually handled by black bush people), seeking big tuskers in the wild for a safari company. Soon he was able

Steven Tors (center) standing with the pilot and mechanic in front of the
helicopter used for rounding up animals in Namibia

to pass the difficult test that qualified him as a licensed hunting guide — he may be the youngest man to do so. A hunting
guide is responsible not only for directing the safari but also for
the safety of his clients and workers; he must be a leader and
a father figure — and now, at age twenty-three, Steve is already both.

But I have jumped ahead. As you can see, Steve did not
readjust to life in California; he had fallen in love with Africa.
He told me that that was the only place he wanted to live — in
the wilderness, where there are rhinos, elephants, and lions,
where the sky is full of bright stars unsullied by smog or city
lights.

Luckily for Steve, my good friend Jan Oelofse, one of the
great animal experts, had just bought twenty thousand acres of

neglected land in his native South-West Africa (Namibia), with the intention of starting a private game reserve. So I sent Steve, and later Pete, to Africa to assist him. They lived in tents and worked all through the daylight hours, seven days a week, surrounding the land with fence so they could capture and breed exotic antelopes such as the Cape oryx, greater kudu, eland, and hartebeest, as well as mountain zebras and giraffes. In time they built, with their own hands, a beautiful house and a dam. A lake was formed by the dam, which made possible a wild bird sanctuary. Together, Jan Oelofse and my boys created a paradise. Eventually, Steve became Jan's junior partner and part owner of the game reserve, which is now our home.

Jan is the toughest man I have ever met, and he has made Steve just as tough. That is, they are tough physically, yet gentle in every other way. It is possible that all of my boys learned something about physical courage from the Masai. They were present once when nine morans (young Masai warriors) came to my camp seeking first aid; all had been badly wounded in a skirmish with another tribe. In a demonstration of extraordinary bravery, not one of the warriors uttered a sound or even flinched when I poured surgical alcohol, the only disinfectant I had in quantity, into their deep wounds.

Later, whenever my sons were injured, they exercised Masai-like determination to overcome pain, and it seems this magically helped their wounds heal faster as well. Once, while taming wild animals for a Hollywood movie, Peter was seriously wounded. The ten-inch scar he now carries on his back required more than a hundred stitches, and the surgeon told him that the healing would take at least three weeks. But in five days Peter had healed, and three weeks later he was with me in the Orinoco jungle as a stunt coordinator, doing strenuous physical work. Likewise, Steve was accidentally shot one day while catching game. He nearly lost his leg, but a week later he was back on the farm, corralling game again. Another time, an oryx speared Steve's hand with its saberlike horn and made a hole through his palm. The helicopter pilot wanted to fly him immediately to the nearest hospital, a hundred miles away; but Steve simply disinfected the wound and went right back to his catching. The hand healed on its own in no time. Do I sound like a proud boasting father? I am.

Thirty years ago, wild animals were captured for zoos by shooting the mothers, who were too dangerous, and then catching the young ones. Then the hypodermic rifle was invented by an American, Red Palmer. This enabled narcotics to be shot into the animals, which made the capture more humane. However, it was difficult to load or handle a creature like a rhino or a buffalo when it revived — and also mighty dangerous. So a description of life on Jan Oelofse's reserve is incomplete without an explanation of his unique method of catching wild game.

I met Jan in Zululand, where he was a game control officer.

Jan Oelofse and a hyena

Game control, at the time, meant that since the land could support only a certain number of animals, the rest had to be shot.

Jan hated to kill animals, and so he found a way to catch them easily. He discovered that animals will not stampede through plastic walls, even if the walls are made of the flimsiest material. His solution was to nail a circle of inexpensive plastic to trees, leaving an opening that could be drawn closed very quickly, like a curtain. Thus he created a corral hidden behind bushes and trees. Jan, on horseback, would chase the animals into this plastic-walled enclosure. As soon as they were inside, they would stop, confused. This gave his men enough time to close the curtain. Strangely, none of the animals ever tried to break through the plastic walls. They were afraid of the unknown.

Next, Jan would drive a big truck close to the outside of the wall. The men would let down a ramp from the truck and erect plastic walls on both sides of the ramp. Then Jan would cut an opening in the wall of the plastic corral. On the opposite side, someone would enter the enclosure and, merely by his presence, scare the animals. Seeing an opening, they would immediately turn in that direction and begin to stampede — right up the ramp and into the truck. When the truck was filled with captive zebras or impalas, the tailgate was closed. The trapped animals were ready to be transported to other pastures.

Jan's method stopped the killings by game control; and selling the surplus animals to other game parks or private farms made the undertaking profitable for the parks department. The Oelofse method became world famous, and now others have learned how to use it.

While Jan was establishing his own game reserve, he set up his plastic corral in places where farmers wanted to rid their land of wild animals. He caught species after species. By then he was herding the animals, not on horseback, but with a helicopter. He would fly above while my son Steve erected the plastic enclosures and closed the curtain. This is how they caught more than two thousand animals for the farm. These

Jan Oelofse as a game warden in Tanganyika (now Tanzania)

animals live in the wild, are never touched by hand, and breed beautifully.

Like Jan, I am against hunting on principle. Still, we have had to accept that we are in the business of breeding near-extinct wild animals in a place where the vegetation is sparse. We need only one bull for fifty females. Any more bulls, then, would simply eat up the food that should be reserved for the mothers and their calves. To have a good breeding herd, we must rid ourselves of the useless males. For this reason, Oelofse now allows hunters on the game farm. But they pay handsomely for the privilege of getting rid of our bull surplus, and we put this money toward further conservation. Emotionally I dislike the thought of killing any healthy animal, but rationally I know Jan is right. I also know that if a hunter merely wounds an animal, Jan or my son will put it out of its misery at once.

Unlike me, my sons Steve and Peter like to hunt, especially birds. But they shoot only what we and our African workers can eat. The African black people live on cornmeal, which they call *posho,* and they are not fond of our kind of food. However, as with any humans, their bodies require protein, and they always welcome the antelope meat brought in by the boys.

Steve and my second son, Peter, are very different from each other. Steve is a loner who is happiest with a few close friends. He dislikes being in big cities. Skiing is his great passion, and when he visits the United States, he spends a month in Sun Valley. Peter, on the other hand, loves people and enjoys city life just as much as wildlife. In fact, Pete's problem is that he likes almost everything. While Steve is dedicated to wildlife management, Peter is also intrigued by deep sea diving, and he may even become a professional diver. He also loves music and has some talent for it. Mostly he loves good living; and he has a special talent for making friends with everyone, human and animal, everywhere.

I took Pete to meet my friend Vivian Bristow, who owns 20,000 acres in Rhodesia, near the ruins of ancient Zimbabwe. Vivian's land is often used by European film companies as a location for Tarzan-style movies, and tame animals as well as wild herds live there. To my great surprise, Pete was fully accepted by the wild animals on the Bristow range — he even walked unharmed among a pride of lions that had previously killed two people.

Pete's skill at making friends with snakes is also quite extraordinary. Once when we were making a film in the Orinoco jungle, Stan Brock, the cohost of *Wild Kingdom,* caught a beautiful tiger snake and gave it to Pete. The natives warned him to be extremely careful, for those snakes, though nonpoisonous, are extremely aggressive. The next day Pete walked with the snake around his neck and slept with him at night.

His lack of fear of animals probably could be traced to an incident on the Mara River when he was sixteen. He was fishing alone, sitting on a rock. He did not see any animals around, but the hour arrived when most animals come to the river, dehydrated from the blazing sun. Suddenly, he found himself surrounded by elephants, buffaloes, and hippos. He had learned

Peter Toro in Rhodesia (*Photo Hank Maartens*)

enough from me not to move — a nonmoving human is very seldom a target for an attack. This was Pete's test, and, alone, unarmed, among a number of potentially dangerous animals, he passed it. When he walked back to the camp in the evening and told me his experience, I knew he was now baptized, as I was. He had faced the moment of truth. When you realize that you are part of nature, that you are not a stranger in strange lands, the African wilderness becomes your territory.

The boys learned many lessons from Africa, but a crucial one — one they learned well — was that staying calm, avoiding panic in trying situations, is essential to survival. At one time, we lived on a coffee plantation north of Nairobi, and the boys made friends with our black neighbors and their children. But there was a tribal dispute, and one of the workers they knew well got drunk one evening and attacked his fellow workers and neighbors with his *panga* (a sharp knife similar to a machete). Steve and Pete disarmed the dangerous man and then saved him from being lynched by the others. Meanwhile, David and I drove the wounded, who were suffering from deep cuts and slashes, to the nearest hospital. David's twelve-year-old black friend, Jorege, was one of the victims. Like the young

Masai warriors I mentioned earlier, Jorege did not shed a single tear nor utter a sound while the surgeon sutured his badly lacerated arm. David, also twelve at the time, demonstrated his courage, too, that night. After his friend had been treated, David on his own escorted him in the pitch dark back to his *shamba* (his home), a mile away.

After the sudden death of my wife, Dave was my greatest concern.

He was only nine years old at the time of her death, and so, while I was not very worried for the older boys and let them go off on safaris and stay with new friends, I kept David with me all the time.

I was committed to go on several filming expeditions, so young Dave was exposed to even more adventures than his brothers were. On my first snake expedition, for example, when we staged a fight between a snake and a mongoose, David had to throw the snake into the ring for the camera to film it. And when I was filming on the Nile, he was with me when a bull hippo tried to climb into our boat and turn us over. He took all this quite nonchalantly.

David also learned early about the different values that human life can be given. In 1972 I rented a farm on the slopes of Mount Kenya and used this place as our headquarters for our *Encyclopedia of Wildlife* filming. David's special friend there was a little Kikuyu girl with whom he frequently played. Once we were away for a few weeks in Uganda. When we returned, he looked for his playmate — only to be told that the little girl was dead. He could not understand it. He came to me for help. I learned that the little girl had had a sore throat and high fever but no one had called a doctor. The dispensary was only a mile down the road, but no one made an effort to get her there. No one seemed to care that she had died — there were too many children on the farm.

When David returned to the United States, he grew disappointed with the schools. Although he liked his teachers and made many friends, he felt that he was not learning enough there. Having traveled far, he realized how little the children and the teachers know about the world outside the United States. The next time he visited Steve in South-West Africa, on his summer vacation, he called me and told me that he thought he could get a better education there, and, with my permission, he would like to enroll and finish school in Windhoek. I granted it to him.

To my great surprise, he liked the school and the discipline. Reveille at 5:30 A.M., classes starting at 7:00, supervised study periods and sports till 8:30 P.M. The change in David was extraordinary. He learned and read more in one year than he had in the previous ten. I could talk to him about Bismarck, Garibaldi, or Cavour. Most students in American schools cannot even identify them. He has become a gentleman and a sportsman, disciplined and polite to everybody. He has friends everywhere. He is determined to become a helicopter pilot or a bush pilot in Africa and fly for his brothers. If the time comes when white people are no longer wanted there, he plans to return to the United States and join the Air Force. Often I think of what would have happened to my sons if I had left them in Los Angeles instead of taking them to Africa. The soft lives, the drug culture, the spoiled friends, the generation gap — how would it all have affected them?

Recently when I was interviewed by a newspaper correspondent, I was asked what I consider to be my most important accomplishment. My answer was, "I have three sons who are not afraid of anything." I could have added that they love me as much as I love them. Can I ask for more?

5 Among the Camel People

My sons and I regressed five thousand years in human history when we visited the land between Somalia, Ethiopia, and Kenya, where only camels and goats and a few tribes of nomadic people survive. We learned about human endurance, life in its most primitive form, and about simple people preserving freedom and dignity, qualities most civilized people are slowly losing. We learned that there are people who refuse to give up even when nature's most cruel forces turn against them, when the desert is littered with human and animal skeletons, and when there is no water and no hope.

I have traveled around the earth many times, but I must say I have never seen a more tortured landscape than the Lake Rudolf area. The topography is a mixture of barren desert, extinct volcanoes, lava flows, and lava dust. The soil is so hard and parched that, even if rain fell, the land would be unable to absorb the water. On our trip, in 1974, we drove through the Chalbi Desert. A few years before, a great rainfall had in fact transformed the desert into a lake; but the heat and high winds eventually evaporated the water and returned the area to its sere condition. By the time we passed through, the earth had again forgotten how the cool rain feels. The rocks are so sharp that driving a few hundred miles may mean the end of four new truck tires, and the lava will settle inside the carburetor and distributor no matter how well sealed off they are. In fact, no one tries to cross this area by car unless he is an explorer or trapper and has plenty of spare parts and provisions. The army and police travel in convoys, but generally they avoid the arid lands or go only as far as Marsabit, where the road ends.

As we looked around in the shriveling heat, someone said, "It could be a backdrop for the staging of Dante's *Inferno*." True; everything looked as if it had been created by angry gods. It is a land without roads, and there is no contact with the outside world, even by radio — on the bottom of the great Rift Valley, the signals are blocked by high mountains.

During World War II, when the Italians were in Ethiopia and the British in Kenya, neither power wanted to hold this area. It was a hell, and possessing it meant only unwanted responsibilities. This attitude still prevails; and thus, most of the civilized world is unaware of the existence of this inhuman region.

The Gabra, Rendile, Turkana, and Boran tribes crisscross this desert with their camels in search of vegetation, rain clouds, and water holes. When they find a good water hole with a few palm trees or thorn bushes around it, they may unload their camels, erect their huts, and stay there until the conditions change. I've seen water holes blown dry by the strong winds in a few hours.

The nomad tribes touched me more than any other group of primitive people I had met during all my previous expeditions.

The nomads in the southern part of the Sahara are striking — black like the Negro but with sharply chiseled faces like those of the Nilotic people. They are tall and straight, as though they were carved from black granite. The men are handsome, with lean sinewy muscles; the women, beautiful and proud, their blouses, necks, arms, and ears adorned with jewelry and ornaments of their own designs, probably fashioned from old tin cans and other metal scraps.

These people must have come down to that forgotten hidden desert under terrible stress, pursued or driven out by other

The nomads on the march (*Photo by Jerome Kurtz*)

tribes. In order to learn to survive there in Hell's Corner, many or most of them had to perish. They took along their livestock, of which only goats and camels were fit enough to survive in that land of vertical sun rays, sixty-mile-an-hour desert winds, and minimum water and roughage.

The camels can go without water for about fifteen days between water holes. But this is possible only when there is browsing material along the way. When the desert is dry, about seven days is the limit of the camel. We were quite surprised to note that the goats have adapted so that they can keep up with camels in this waterless existence.

The camels of these nomads are quite different from those of the Tuaregs, Berbers, and Bedouins. These are gentle camels. They are pampered members of the group because men are totally dependent on them for survival. Nearly the entire food intake of these nomads comes from the milk of the camel. If their camels die, the tribe is wiped out by famine. These nomads do not ride on their camels. They use them only for milking and for carrying their meager belongings. Loading the camels is an art in itself. Sections of the nomads' huts are stripped off to provide protection for the camels' backs. Then the tent poles are attached vertically to the camels' sides; and finally camel-hide coverings are tied between the poles. In this manner, one camel can carry the essential parts of three huts. The huts, when put together, look like beehives made of poles, sticks, camels' hides, and grass mats.

The camels, when loaded, look oddly like land-bound ships with sails unfurled. But a caravan outlined against the sinking red disc of the sun, or against the rising full moon, looks breathtakingly like a scene from the Bible brought to life. And as a matter of fact, these tribes have not changed a great deal since biblical times.

Their endurance, their performance against tremendous odds, seems superhuman. They have accepted a mode of life that a Westerner could stand for only a few days before dropping dead from exhaustion. We filmed there in the dry season, when it was the hottest. The nomads follow their fast-stepping camels on foot, while the animals look for some kind of nourishment from palm fronds, tree bark, thorn brush, or cactus. The women, including mothers with children tied to their backs or breasts, follow directly behind the camels. Next come the dignified warriors, carrying sharp spears and daggers, dressed in their white burnooses, which always looked clean. And last, but no less incredible, come the crippled and other disabled, among whom we've seen people with clubfeet and with broken legs. They know that falling behind the rest would mean losing their lives. And so they manage to keep up . . . keep up . . . keep up with the fast pace of the others.

The dignity of these people, the simplicity of their lifestyle, moved all of us — how unlike Western people they are. They know not to care about tomorrow. Today is the only day they can be sure of, for the desert has betrayed them time and again. Normally, two rains fall each year, maintaining a marginal vegetation that sustains their camels and goats and consequently themselves. For two years they had waited in vain. They were unaware that the drought was not a local phenomenon. Hundreds of miles north, on a five-thousand-mile front from Senegal to Eritrea, the Sahara was on the march. Twenty million people, with their cattle, camels, sheep, and goats, were in danger. The edge of the Sahara, with just enough vegetation to sustain life, kept turning into sand dunes and parched barren earth. Our expedition concentrated on the southernmost part of this arid zone and the nomads who lived there, the Gabra.

We attempted to discover what kind of help a small group of trained scientists could offer the local nomads and to make a record on film. Of course, the first step was to learn more about the nomads themselves. Incredibly, I could find nothing written about them when I searched the libraries for information. We would have to find out on our own. What was the possibility of resettling them near a permanent water hole? How feasible would it be to teach them some form of agriculture, such as growing date palms by digging irrigation ditches? The never-ceasing desert wind looked to us like an excellent source of energy, not necessarily for generating electricity, but for driving water into irrigation canals and pumping it up from underground water tables.

We soon learned that the nomadic tribes' refusal to settle down had something to do with women's lib, Sahara-style. Most of these tribes are Mohammedan. Muslim women in inhabited areas, villages and port cities, have no freedom. They live behind veils, hidden from the rest of society, in semiconfinement.

The nomad women, however, live in freedom. Unveiled, they lead the camels and do the chores. They are not treated as chattel but are outspoken equals of their warrior husbands. For them, settling down and creating a village would mean returning to slavery. Their direction would come from the mosque police rather than from the rainclouds they must follow and the water holes they must locate. The nomads may be underfed and abused by nature, but they live as free people.

As the Gabra crisscross the desert, they disregard the borderlines of Ethiopia, northern Kenya, and Somalia. There are no border signs, and even the concept of separate countries may not be clear to them at all. The Kenyan Gabra may not at all perceive that less than four hundred miles south there is a metropolis named Nairobi, with street lights, skyscrapers, and over a hundred thousand automobiles.

To begin our expedition, we flew from that city in a small aircraft and carefully made our approach to land on the flat desert surface near North Horr, the only so-called settlement in the 10,000-square-mile area that is the Chalbi Desert. All the maps show it; but locating it—even from the air, in daylight—is not easy, because the airport consists of a windsock planted in the sand. For this reason and because the high winds can easily flip a plane during landing or takeoff, most

A rest halt on the march (*Photo by Jerome Kurtz*)

pilots dislike flying in this area. It would be difficult to spot a wreck among the lava rocks, and no crash survivor would live long in the fiery heat and the strong winds that accelerate dehydration. A further drawback: fuel depots, where a search plane could refuel, are scarce.

The water tables in this territory are covered by a limy stratum under the sand, so North Horr is the source of many slightly salty water holes. But here even salty water is welcome, and it lures many thousands of camels and nomads, who passed our tented camp every morning.

During our stay in the desert, we found the nights nearly as hot as the days, for lava retains heat better than any other formation. The only comfortably cool time was between four and six in the morning. After that, the intense heat would rise and we would begin to suffer again. But the early morning hours were also the hours of the snake. While the air was still cool the snakes looked for refuge from the rays of the desert sun. They sought shade under palm fronds or under tent flaps or even in the latrines. They would burrow into the relatively cool sand or into some hollow, such as the inside of a shoe.

Among the snake population is the small but deadly saw-scaled viper, for whose venom most people say there is no antidote. We learned to be very careful of our footsteps. Interestingly, despite the fact that the many children run around barefoot in this area infested with scorpions, vipers, and puff adders, very few are bitten. This, again, would indicate that most venomous creatures are nonaggressive. To be bitten, one must step on them by accident or touch them.

Contrary to many warnings, I found that most tribes were not hostile to our intrusion. They were just as fascinated with us as we with them. Our gadgetry — binoculars, cameras, small and large planes, ice machines — must have paralleled our own notions of seeing visitors from another planet. Many tribes — Turkana, Boran, Rendile — walked out of their way, perhaps even a hundred miles, to catch a glimpse of us. We met only one nomad, a Gabra, who had an elementary education in English, and we immediately hired him as our interpreter.

Mingling with them, I found that their languages do not contain many words. They are a silent people, unacquainted with certain human responses and expressions we take for granted. The men and young women accepted our small gifts wordlessly, without thanking us; but we came to realize that people who have never in their lives received anything for free cannot articulate gratitude. Likewise, they have few expressions for joy. But when my sons built them a windmill to pump water — a miracle they had never seen before — they sang the only song they knew, in worship of the windmill.

The next biggest miracles were taking their pictures with our Polaroid Land camera and recording their voices. They were both fascinated and amused by their own images, and they burst into hearty laughter when we replayed their voices. This helped us a great deal in overcoming their hostility and fear of unknown objects such as our movie cameras.

Only the older women of the tribes did not like us, because they tended to be extremely superstitious and to distrust all unfamiliar things. They forbade us to photograph their huts or themselves as they tended their camels, even when we offered them food, money, and gifts.

The tribe we filmed, the Gabra, grazed their camels about ten miles from our tents. Every morning they walked ten miles to meet us. At 8:00 A.M., I would begin to film them. By 11:00 A.M. I would send them back to their home grounds, another ten-mile walk. Late in the afternoon, almost every day, they would appear again, after covering the same distance without their camels, to observe the activities of ours that intrigued them so much. My associates often bought some of their trinkets for a few shillings. They would then take this money to the Somali trader who had a shop in an adobe hut and exchange it for whatever goods he might have available that they

David Tors, at age 12, helps in the filming (*Photo by Jerome Kurtz*)

could afford. The merchandise varied from week to week — once, a case of Pepsi-Cola, next, some cloth from Nairobi or a bag of maize.

The Gabras' economy depends completely on camels' milk. A normal female camel will give about two gallons of milk a day. To ensure that there will be enough milk to make the warm yogurtlike concoction that is the nomads' staple food, all four of the camel's teats are tied off. At feeding time, one is untied for the baby camel to suckle; and at milking time, the other three are untied to provide human sustenance. When the grazing is satisfactory and there is enough water — conditions we did not observe while we were there — the nomads can take their surplus goats, camels, and curdled milk, and trade these in North Horr for maize, cloth, tea, and sugar. When there is a surplus of male camels, some of them are castrated, which causes them to grow fat. Then, when the going gets rough and the supply of curdled milk dwindles in the nomads' gourds, they will slaughter one or two of the fatted camels. The meat, which is sliced into long strips and dried, is their reserve food supply.

Hoping to find a way to help the Gabra during the drought, we tried to feed their hungry camels with oats. To our great surprise and disappointment, the animals rejected this food. They had never before eaten grain, and so, not knowing what it was, they refused to taste it.

Although a gentle coexistence exists between man and beast within each tribe, the same is not true of man and man among the tribes. When a tribe can take another tribe by surprise it may rob it of its livestock. Recently, a group of Turkana had been raided by the Samburu. Then the Samburu evacuated their own huts and took off with their own as well as the stolen animals. The next night, a tribe of Rendile nomads passed the empty huts and decided to sleep there. On this night, the vengeful Turkana, believing they had caught the thieving Samburu, attacked and killed thirty-seven Rendile. Thirty-seven mutilated bodies were eventually piled up in a police lorry. That incident did not even rate an article in the Nairobi papers.

Recently, a police post has been erected on two sand dunes as a base for a camel patrol to protect the Kenyan nomads from armed raids by Ethiopian or Somali nomads who cross the borders, attack the Kenyan tribes, and steal their stock. These raids are usually very bloody because the raiders slaughter everyone in the camp, including children, to eliminate any chance of identification. The day before we arrived in Chalbi, Ethiopian raiders had wiped out a Boran settlement, leaving seventy dead.

During these raids the Kenyan nomads are at a disadvantage, for they are forbidden to have firearms. The Somalis and many Ethiopians, on the other hand, have Russian or Chinese submachine guns, which were given to them for guerilla action. Thus the Kenyan tribes most often suffer the devastating losses.

After such raids, the North Horr police, riding camels, attempt pursuit and retribution. But the terrain here is usually too difficult for successful pursuit, and the culprits are able to reach their own borders. So the bloody raids go on.

During our stay in the desert, we visited a Catholic mission and became acquainted with the Italian padre who built it, the Peace Corps worker who helped him, and the German nun who runs the dispensary all by herself.

The problem faced by the padre personalizes the whole system of foreign aid. This kind man who dug the wells and built the mission, the school, and the dispensary, receives financial aid from the German government. He does not preach to the nomad; he does not even say that he is a Catholic. His religion consists entirely of helping people. He is equipped to serve lunches to the 280 hungry children who come to the mission for their daily food rations. The lives of these people depend on the padre and the German aid.

But this fine, unselfish man was just as tortured as the landscape. Talking with him, I could feel his tremendous doubts. Is he doing the right thing? What will happen to all the children

Nomad warriors (*Photo by Jerome Kurtz*)

after the tribes move on or North Horr runs out of water? The children are used to having daily meals and the shade of the adobe mission. How will they resist the rays of the sun, starvation, being without water for days? I remember one day when we looked into the padre's own larder. His personal food supply consisted of one potato, one onion, and one carrot.

We left him and the nomads of the Chalbi Desert with regret. After having lived so closely with these people, my sons and I felt that we would never again complain about anything. In their marginal existence, their future depends solely on atmospheric conditions. As the desert marches on, it may bury them forever without their disappearance ever being mentioned in our home town papers. They carry no birth certificates, they do not have a written language, and when a tribe is wiped out by another tribe, no one takes notice.

In the belief of many tribes, the Emerald Sea (as Lake Rudolf, now called Lake Turkana, is nicknamed) is where the world ends; if one were to go beyond its far shore, one would fall off this flat earth. Perhaps such beliefs as these keep them saner than we are. The thought of infinity — trying to imagine galaxy beyond galaxy beyond galaxy — staggers the mind. It must be a comfort to know that the end of the world is at Lake Rudolf.

6   In Cold Sweat

LIONS ARE THE MOST HANDSOME CREATURES in nature — and the most unpredictable. I will never forget the day in the Samburu Game Reserve, in Kenya, when I was alone in an open jeep, driving through the dry bush country. I heard something move behind a thorn bush, and I stopped the jeep and stood up. I did not have to wait too long. A beautiful, tawny, sleek lioness moved out of the bush and walked up to the car. She rubbed her back and rump against the bumper, then scratched her side against the fender. She never noticed my presence. I must confess I was somewhat perturbed by this. What was I to her? A rodent? A baboon? I wasn't even worthy enough to kill or eat. She was a queen and, to her, I was nothing.

In Africa, lions often moved into our campsite. They chewed up our camp chairs, turned over small tables, and at the same time refused to find us worth noticing. However, when they are feeding on a zebra or a wildebeest, it is not advisable to approach them. They chase away the hyenas, jackals, and vultures. They insist on privacy while eating, so I try to keep far away from them during their mealtime.

I learned a long time ago that actually we are not on the menu of the average lion. Lions prefer larger animals like antelopes. Sometimes they will even take on buffalo and giraffes, but in these fights, the lions are often the losers. One night, in the Tsavo National Park, I heard the bloodcurdling sounds of a terrible fight. The next morning, not far from the camp, I found the gored carcass of a full-maned lion and the body of a bull buffalo, both predator and prey dead from the loss of blood. Why would a lion challenge such a formidable adversary when the savanna is full of easy kills like the wildebeest, zebra, impala, and hartebeest? It must be a question of pride — or stupidity.

Lions will sometimes attack men gratuitously, but not often. Just as a cat will pounce on a rolling ball, a lion may jump on anything that runs away from him. His instinct to attack a runaway target is imprinted in him and does not follow logic. My soundman Jimmy Chapman, for example, was killed by a semi-tame lion when Jimmy ran from him. On the other hand, when Dr. Livingstone was attacked by a lion, he did the proper thing and did not move. He was seriously injured but he was not killed. A lion is quite harmless when he is taking a siesta because he does not want to be bothered. While driving in the Serengeti Plain, I once passed two beautiful black-maned lions resting in the short grass, and I wanted to photograph them. My sons and my assistant made all kinds of noises — slamming car doors, honking horns — anything to make them react, short of throwing stones at them. Neither of the lions paid any attention to us. Even when I got out of the car and approached them, they disregarded us totally, shut their eyes, and dozed off.

There was one time, however, when things were different, when I was followed all day by a large female, when in a cold sweat I anticipated an attack, when I learned more about lions than I ever hoped to learn.

It started in the Serengeti Plain. Dr. Murray Watson, an ecologist, allowed me to go along with him in his Piper Super Cub when he went out to take an animal census. It was an unforgettable day and an unforgettable sight.

Millions of animals were migrating from the bone-dry

Serengeti Plain to Lake Victoria and the Masai Mara Game Reserve in search of water and green grass. The vision took me
back millions of years to when animals ruled the world, and
our ancestors, the apelike humanoids, were hiding in caves
and coves or dense forests in hope of being less visible, just as
gorillas behave today on the slopes of the Virunga volcano or
the Ruwenzori Mountains. I felt elated to observe nature in this
primal form, the parade of each species, the wildebeests moving in single file by the tens of thousands, followed by zebras,
buffaloes, a herd of elephants. Elsewhere, a troupe of giraffes
advanced, flanked by lions, predators following the prey. Some
people call this migration the eighth wonder of the world. To
me it is the greatest wonder.

Different animals evolve to take advantage of different oppor-
tunities in nature. The browsers, the bush eaters, the grazers,
the grass eaters, animals with long necks, animals with short
necks, animals with stripes, animals in camouflage suits, animals with horns of different shapes and designs, all are endowed with an instinct that will guide them to the right place
at the right time to assure the survival of their newborn.

The next morning, at first light, I left our camp to intercept
this incredible migration and study their behavior during such
mass movement. Lions were visible everywhere. From the
plane, we counted 104 lions, moving along in peaceful coexistence with the antelopes, zebras, and giraffes. Lions feed in the
night, and the grass eaters are aware that their enemies are not
hungry during the day, so they accept their presence.

Later, studying a behavioral phenomenon among the plains
animals, I drove among the wild herds in my Land-Rover and
noticed that while a hundred gazelles would break into a fast
gallop as my car approached, a few would stand still, undis-
turbed and unafraid. The same held true with the hartebeests,
zebras, and others. My interest was in the different tempera-
ments and degrees of excitability of the individual animals.

While I watched the migrating herds, I paid no attention to

my thermostat. Suddenly my radiator began to steam and my car was in serious trouble. I stopped and opened the hood while four pairs of lion eyes watched me from the bush as I diagnosed the fact that my water pump had committed suicide. It was an unpleasant discovery in ninety-degree heat, at least twenty-two miles from our camp. I was not on a road where I could count on other cars coming along. I had no weapon, no food, no radio. My only choice was to walk back to the camp, crossing through the migrating herds with lions on the flanks, not to mention elephants, rhinos, and hyenas. There was also the danger of sunstroke. I had no hat, and most of the land was open to the sky. A sunstroke can be as fatal as an attack by a lion if not treated immediately. And I had still another problem. I had recently fractured some of my vertebrae, and so I was not in my best physical condition. Was I scared? Yes! But I had to start at once to reach help before nightfall. Most of the predators, especially the hyenas, like to eat people at night, and I didn't cherish the idea of being eaten by a hyena.

As soon as I began my long walk, I heard the yellow grass rustling behind me. I turned and looked. There was an enormous female lion following me, just sauntering behind me. I knew that I must not run or I might provoke an attack. When a 500-pound body pounces on a human back, something is bound to give. I knew what I had to do. I must disregard her and do nothing that would excite her, but I could not help thinking about my friend who was killed by a lion, and this did not do much for my morale.

I tried to think positively, persuading myself that to be killed by a lion is not the worst thing that could happen to me. I have witnessed many lion kills, and most of them are immediate. I thought that, since I am a zoologist, it would be quite stylish to end that way — both stylish and swift. It would come at the peak of my career. No hospitals. No senility. No suffering. It would be a distinguished end to my life as an explorer: "Ivan Tors, died at age fifty-seven in Masai territory, killed by a lion."

I liked the way it sounded. I was less scared than before. It was settled in my mind: today I will be eaten by a lion and I will die in style.

Suddenly I noticed a nine-foot-long python slithering in front of my feet. Impulsively I jumped over the snake. The python struck because I had frightened her. But she missed my leg. Then I realized my own stupidity. My quick move could have startled the lion and she could have jumped on me. I looked behind me, but I did not see the lion. Either the grass was too high or she had decided on a detour.

I continued my journey through the high grass. A herd of hartebeests blocked my path. It would be quite easy for one of these giant antelopes to run a man down, but in their genetic memory, they still retain the print of the great fangs of the saber-toothed tiger from a time when fighting was useless and flight was the only escape. Their enemies, including the lions and the leopards, developed fangs and claws, and the antelopes themselves developed powerful legs and split toes to carry them over soft grounds with considerable speed. But antelopes have also come to understand lions better than any scholar has, and so have found another way to save their hides.

Lions have formed the habit, during the many millions of years of successful existence, of surprising their prey. This means stalking them from behind against the wind and jumping on their backs when an attack is least suspected — usually breaking the back of the prey. Antelopes, for their part, have learned that frontal attack is unlikely and that spotting a lion and not running is the safest tactic. If an antelope herd sees a lion, they usually turn toward the lion and stare him down. The lion, thus discovered, becomes confused, and then disappears to try his luck on another herd of antelopes that perhaps will remain unaware of his presence.

When the hartebeests in front of me did not run away, but stood staring past me, I knew that the lioness, my faithful if unnerving companion, was still behind me — it was she who was holding their attention. I continued on until I reached a riverine forest. I could no longer see my pursuer, but giraffes were staring at me from their high vantage point, and suddenly I heard something that I didn't like. I looked to my left, where the strange sound originated, and there he was, a huge red-maned lion, taking his noontime nap and snoring like mad. He looked like a stuffed toy, but I knew he was packed with dynamite. As I watched him with some degree of anxiety, a tsetse fly landed on my nose and bit me. My sharp slap scared the giraffes away, but luckily it did not awaken the dreaming lion.

Since it was too hot for me in the open savanna, I entered the wooded area — and there awaiting me was another surprise. A herd of Cape buffaloes with the same idea had sought shelter in the shaded area that I was headed for.

The buffalo is considered man's most dangerous adversary on the African continent. More hunters have been killed by buffaloes than by lions, leopards, and elephants combined. I moved very slowly, parallel with their column, never toward them. They stopped browsing and eyed me with their bloodshot, villainous eyes. Suddenly they broke into a gallop, not toward me but away from me. I followed them cautiously, relying on the thought that they had decided that I was no menace. But then they abruptly stopped and all stared in my direction again, as though they had changed their minds. I looked behind me. As with the hartebeests it was not I who was the target of their gaze; my lioness was still behind me after all, accompanying me back to the river.

I had walked too many hours and I was dehydrated. I was almost at the point of being indifferent to the danger. I picked up a twig and took a bearing with my watch. By halving the arc made by the shadow of the twig on my watch, I confirmed that I was headed in the right direction, and so I continued through the grass, avoiding the more unpredictable wooded area.

I walked about fifteen minutes and reached a tree. I felt weak and I wanted to rest for a few minutes in the shade. Suddenly, an ominous growl sent a rush of adrenalin through my veins. I turned around. There were two lions behind me.

They seemed to be behaving strangely, as if they were in a fighting mood. Looking for escape, I climbed up the tree in front of me but the branch I reached for snapped, and I fell ten feet — onto a sharp rock. I didn't feel the pain at first because I was too scared, thinking that the lions would be on top of me any second. I was wrong. The lions were tangling limbs, the male on top of the female. There they were, just two feet away from me, mating. Lion lovemaking, as I then observed from close up, is accompanied by biting, growling, and a lot of macho behavior. I had been snubbed again. They did not give a damn about the human baboon.

In my fall, I had reinjured my broken vertebrae and smashed my watch. I was in pain, and from here on, I could only follow my nose. But none of this stopped me from getting away from the amorous pair and continuing toward the camp. I had only one motivation, and that was to get back and relieve my thirst.

As I kept walking in the late afternoon hour, the lioness passed me unexpectedly on my right and took a position on a high mound. I soon realized what she was interested in. At that moment, a pack of wild dogs appeared from a clump of trees. The African hunting dog is as ugly as the lion is beautiful. He is not big, not strong, and he has ragged spotted fur of many colors. Lone dogs could not survive in the African savanna because hyenas and leopards would eat them for breakfast, but a hunting pack is a dangerous force and cannot be challenged by hyenas, leopards, or lions. In fact, as a pack, they are the best-organized hunters of the veldt.

That afternoon I had a graphic demonstration of this. The target of the pack was a five-hundred-pound wildebeest, which has deadly hooves and deadly horns. The lead dog, who could not have weighed more than forty-five pounds, rushed the antelope, attacking it head-on, and bit through its nostrils. With a mighty jerk, he pulled the wildebeest's head down and threw the animal off balance. With the dog's fangs firmly embedded in the beast's nose, it could neither kick nor gore, and no matter how hard it shook its head, it could not dislodge the lead dog. At the same moment, three other dogs attacked the antelope, tearing at its flanks, hamstringing it, immobilizing it. Within seconds, the huge wildebeest was lying on its side, being eaten alive, for the rest of the pack had joined the attackers and were gorging themselves on the hot bloody meat. I was quite positive that the animal did not feel any pain. The unexpected attack, the struggle, and the resulting rush of adrenalin paralyzed and anesthetized it.

With all this excitement I realized I had not paid attention to the lioness. But when I looked at the mound, it was deserted, nor could I spot her anywhere else. She, too, had seen the terrifying and impressive skill with which the wild dogs had made their kill, and she had decided to move on to less precarious ground. I, however, stayed awhile longer to observe the dogs' behavior, and I was rewarded with another example of their cooperation.

When they had eaten their fill, they returned to the nearby hyena hole that was their temporary residence. About fifteen tiny pups, under the watchful eye of a full-grown female, were waiting for them. The lead dog regurgitated his food so that the babysitter dog could eat, and the others regurgitated their food for the pups. It was the most unselfish society I have ever encountered. Nature had taught them that they could survive in competition with other large predators only by full cooperation with one another. The care for their young overshadowed their own hunger. They would then go on another hunt to fill up their own stomachs. I could no longer despise this "despicable" breed. I found something appealing in their lifestyle, even if the antelopes would disagree.

Night would fall any minute, but I was near the river and close to our campsite. The Mara River was surrounded by herds of elephants, buffaloes, waterbucks, hippos, and a few basking crocodiles. I had become a different person since I began my walk in the morning; I was no longer scared. After all, the creatures of the wild had left me alone and allowed me to survive. I was part of the ecosystem.

I was almost at the end of my journey, but I was so dehydrated that I could wait no longer to drink. The Mara River is probably infested with blood flukes, flatworms that carry the disease bilharziasis, which destroys the human kidney. Nevertheless, I dropped onto the ground at a place where the flow of the river was swift, remembering that germs usually cannot survive in fast-flowing water. I washed my face and drank and drank, not caring that it might mean my death. A hippo and a crocodile watched me, but I felt that I was one of them and needn't be afraid. They had had plenty of food that day from the migration crossing the river, and I was not on their menu. Ten minutes later I was back at camp.

It had been the most horrifying and the most beautiful day of my life. I arrived home with new feelings, new understandings, a new outlook. From then on, I belonged among the natural creatures. I was fit to survive!

7 Monsters of the Nile

As a child I used to dream about the Nile. I had read all the books on the exploration of the headwaters, such as the travels of Sir Richard Burton, Sir Samuel Baker, John Speke, and other pioneers, and now, many years later, I was there. I hired a fifty-five-foot powerboat from the Ugandan game department and set off to cover the Victoria Nile. Accompanying me were my ten-year-old son David; my cameraman, John Pearson; his wife and assistant, Jennie; and three Acholi tribesmen, who were our guides. The weather was perfect, the vistas magnificent — Murchison Falls (now Kabarega Falls) in the background and forests bordering the great river, from which elephants, buffaloes, and waterbucks drank. There were giant hippos everywhere, and I counted 650 large crocodiles between Para Lodge and the falls, a distance of ten miles.

As our boat passed a herd of elephants drinking, I told my son how, according to Rudyard Kipling, the elephant got his trunk. The fairy tale related that elephants used to have ordinary noses, but once when an elephant was drinking, a giant crocodile grabbed his nose and pulled and pulled until it became a trunk. As I was telling the story, one of the Acholi boatmen interrupted me, saying that the fairy tale was a lie. He had once seen a crocodile grab the trunk of an elephant and the elephant heave the croc against a tree, breaking its body in two.

So we all stopped worrying about the elephants on the river bank.

The life of a crocodile is not an easy one. Being cold-blooded, the croc cannot regulate body heat internally. He can die from getting too hot and he can die from getting too cold. This is the reason why crocs are always basking on the river banks. When their bodies heat up, they either slide into the water or just place their tails in the water to cool off. Their jaws are often wide open, but this is not because they plan to swallow any-body but because the lower and upper palates offer additional cooling surfaces when it is too hot. At night when it is cooler than 25° Celsius, they leave the banks and warm up in the water. To keep themselves submerged, crocodiles swallow large pebbles to weigh them down, just as we wear belts weighted with lead when we go scuba diving.

In summer, when the rivers dry up, crocodiles aestivate, which is the summer equivalent of hibernation. This means that the crocodiles dig themselves into the sand so that they can be cooled by the cold soil below the surface. In this dor-mant state, they can survive without eating or drinking water for at least six months.

In observing the behavior of the crocodile, I again noticed the similarity between animals and humans. A hungry man will be more motivated toward violence and murder than a well-fed man. The same is true of crocs. A hungry croc is a dangerous croc; one with a full belly is not. Interestingly, it takes less to appease a croc's hunger than it does to appease a man's. This is because warm-blooded animals, from rodents to men, annually have to eat food equal to five hundred times their body weight, while cold-blooded animals can survive on sustenance three or four times their body weight because their metabolism is much slower.

Our Acholi boatmen had indicated that there was no need to fear the crocodiles of the Nile. The reason, I soon discovered, is that the river is teeming with perch, the crocodile's favorite food. The perch there grow to extraordinary sizes, up to 200 pounds, and the crocs find them quite satisfying — enough so that people are not on their regular menu.

When I saw the boatmen wading in the Nile among the crocodiles, I was convinced there was nothing to fear and decided to try an experiment. In the center of the river was a sandbar about a hundred feet long and sixty feet wide. There were twenty-five extremely big crocodiles basking on this small island. I told the guides to take the boat close to the sandbar, and then I jumped to it from the bow.

Testing crocodiles on the sandbar was not the smartest thing to do. I learned later of a friend of mine who had tried the same thing on Lake Rudolf, and now he has a tattoo of 350 stitches on his hip and leg. A small crocodile he had not seen in the bulrushes had been surprised and, out of its own fear, had grabbed him. One thing to know about crocodiles is that they may appear to be asleep but the next second they might twist their deadly jaws ninety degrees and snatch an unsuspecting animal or man.

But my experience on the Nile that day was quite different. As soon as I landed on the sandbar, all but one of the giant crocs skidded into the water. The oldest one, who was the biggest and darkest, simply ignored me and stayed in place, his jaws gaping. This was the first time I realized that in the good old Tarzan films, when Tarzan jumped into the water, the crocs slid into the water not to eat him but because they were frightened by the splash and they sought safety in their normal living space, the river or the lake.

At another time, when I was rafting down the Mara River at migration time, crocs again posed no threat to me. Millions of animals were crossing the river and some of them drowned. In one area, I counted forty-five carcasses. The crocs had their bellies full for months to come.

I should point out here that crocs really do more good than harm. The animals that crocs will grab in a river or a water hole are usually the slow, the old, or the less alert. In this way they improve the herds and the gene pools of other wildlife.

Unfortunately there are those crocs whose behavior does not fit my preceding description of that species' ecologically balanced natural instincts. Just as we have such crazy people as snipers and assassins, so there exist man-eating crocodiles. These are usually mean old crocs who lurk underwater at river fords where natives cross. They may lie in wait at the crossings for months. Then one day they gather the courage to taste a new kind of food and they strike out and grab a child. If the croc likes the taste, he will do it again and again, always at the same spot. The crocodile brain is not very advanced, so crocs tend to act on habit alone. It is easy to find the man-eating crocodile at his usual site and shoot him between the eyes.

I neither love nor hate crocodiles, but I am intrigued by them. They are the last of the large saurians (lizards) to survive to the present age from the time when dinosaurs walked the earth and *Tyrannosaurus Rex* was the bully of the ancient fern forests. After a hundred million years of ruling the earth, why did the giant lizards disappear from the face of the earth? Why did the age of the dinosaurs end so abruptly? And why did the crocodile survive? Scientists speculate on the answers to these mysteries and so do I.

One theory is that, because lizards have no sweat glands, they could not regulate their body temperature by evaporation when the climate changed. The smaller saurians, like the crocodiles, were able to dig into the soil to insulate themselves for long periods of time and so were able to endure the changes; but the giants, weighing tons, had no choice but to remain on the surface and so perished. Another theory is that the saurians from whom the crocodiles descended died along with the giant lizards but some of their eggs remained in suspended animation. Millions of years later, when the weather returned to normal, the eggs hatched and the hatchlings could again cope with life on earth. The eggs of the giant saurians, on the other hand, had been laid on top of the ground, and the newly developed small mammals, like the shrews, ate their eggs. As

Some of the monsters (*Photo by Hank Maartens*)

an added problem, parts of the world experienced flooding, and the behemoths bogged down in the resulting quagmire and drowned. The crocodiles, on the other hand, were physically equipped to handle that situation.

The crocodile's horned, leathery, armorlike hide originally served to protect it from other aggressive saurian dinosaurs. (All of the croc's enemies in the animal world are now extinct.) Crocs are yellowish when young and become darker as they grow older and larger. The oldest and largest crocs we encountered were a dark smoky color. Crocs grow a foot a year until their tenth year, and from then on the growth slows down considerably. Their hind legs are web-footed and larger than their front legs, another dinosaurian characteristic, indicating that they once walked upright. They swim in the water by undulating their long, dragonlike muscular tails. When they want to or need to, they can swim extremely fast. I once observed a mother hippo chasing a croc who had got too close to her baby. The croc's getaway speed was amazing. He skimmed over the water surface as though he were on water-skis. The croc's tail also acts as an effective weapon. With extraordinary agility and

speed, the croc can whip its tail around and knock any creature under a thousand pounds off its feet.

One afternoon, as I was looking through my binoculars, I
could not believe my eyes. In a small cove, I discovered the biggest crocodile I had ever seen. His body, lying on the ground,
seemed nearly four feet high. I ordered the boatmen to tie
up next to the croc. He was big, all right, and old — perhaps as
much as a hundred years old. He was the blackest crocodile I
have ever laid eyes on. He did not pay attention to us at all. We
had a long oar and measured the length of the monster at sixteen feet. I wanted the croc to get up on his legs so that I could
see his size while standing. We thwacked him with our oar.
We threw rocks at him. He took no notice. He was the old man
of the Nile who feared nothing and did not want to be bothered. His size was so enormous that he could have overturned
any normal boat the natives use for fishing, but my boat was
fifty-five feet long and made of steel. Then, suddenly the le-
thargic old saurian moved so fast that he scared us all, and he
disappeared into the water even faster. I will never forget that
creature as long as I live.

At another point in our journey, as we were slowly cruising
along on the Nile, I noticed a crocodile swimming steadily up-
stream. There was something unusual about him — his nostrils were above water. Although crocs usually dive under and
disappear when approached by a boat, this croc did not duck
but kept on swimming in the same direction, as if guided by a
compass. After a mile, I realized what the old bull was after. A
carcass appeared on the horizon and I looked at it through my
binoculars. First it seemed to be a dead hippo. When we got
closer, I realized that it was a dead crocodile. With the white
belly up, it was deceptive. Our croc had smelled the dead croc
miles away, even though the river was full of other scents —
exhaust fumes of boats, water lilies, and the droppings of hippos. This was the first time I realized the excellent sense of
smell of these giant lizards. (I later conducted experiments in
the Everglades and I came to the conclusion that only blood-

hounds are better than crocodiles in tracking down smells.)

I filmed the crocodile in its cannibalistic eating of the carcass. Feeding is itself a chore for crocodiles. When they pull a chunk of meat off their prey with their formidable teeth, they must shake it and soften it before they are able to swallow it. The sharp conical teeth of the croc are replaced by new ones when broken or worn off (just like the teeth of sharks), but crocs do not have mobile tongues. Instead they have an undulating lower palate, which carries the food, assembly-line fashion, to the gullet.

While observing this particular feeding, I learned something more about crocodiles — they are very territorial. Our downstream croc had ventured into the territory of another bull, who interrupted his siesta on the bank and swam to the carcass that had now drifted within his property line. As this somewhat smaller bull approached, the intruder moved away and let the territory-owner feed on the dead croc. When he was finished and had returned to the bank, the intruder then resumed feeding.

There is an order of rank among crocodiles. The stronger bulls bask on the best beaches surrounded by a harem of females. Other large bulls will avoid their territory.

When they mate, crocs show a kind of affection, lying across each other in the water or on the beach. A few months after mating, the female croc will dig a hole on the river bank and lay her eggs. She stays near her eggs until they are matured. The baby crocodiles signal their readiness to leave their eggs by emitting hiccuplike cries. Upon hearing them, the mother uncovers the eggs and the perfectly formed baby crocodiles hatch.

I did not witness the birth of baby crocodiles because I was on the Nile during the wrong month, but my boatman told me that crocodiles show much concern for their young. Snakes do not and turtles do not. The mother croc, however, carries her young on her broad head to sheltered areas, where they can hide and where the rivulets are too narrow for the father to get close. Crocodiles, as I have said, are cannibalistic, and the bulls enjoy eating their own young. In my next incarnation, I refuse to be a crocodile.

While cruising on the Nile, I came across the strangest combination of friends. At a certain bend of the river, I observed a fifteen-foot crocodile basking in the sand, and close to the croc stood a buffalo nibbling on the long grass. The next time we passed the same bend, the two creatures were still together. I made a point of observing these animals every day for a week and they never left each other's company. The buffalo was a bull and must have been banished from the herd by the lead bull. Herd animals do not like to be alone and this bull had chosen this old crocodile to be his friend. As you will read, I have recorded many other such strange companionships.

Another creature I studied on the Nile was the hippopotamus, with its thick, pink skin; very large mouth; sharp, tusk-like canines; and incisors made of fine ivory. Their bodies are enormous, and their anatomy has not changed over the past few million years, proving that they have adapted perfectly to their surroundings — the rivers and lakes of Africa. *Hippopotamus* means "river horse"; this is a misnomer because these creatures are related to the pig, not the horse. The Greek who named them goofed! They are really giant river pigs.

Hippos live in herds of twenty to forty, depending on the strength of the ruling bull. Being clannish and overprotective of their young, these herbivorous grazers are dangerous when man gets too close — as we learned by experience when we tried to get near a herd. The lead bull, sensing a threat, took on our large boat. He attacked us amidships; he hooked his giant tusks into the gunwale, and when he could not turn over the boat, he tried to climb into it. Luckily for us, his tusks broke off and thus his attack was stopped. We got a good scare but also some good film because John Pearson, unafraid as usual, kept the camera running.

Two years later, Dr. Murray Watson and I were rafting down the Mara River in a small rubber raft. When we reached a bend, about fifteen hippo heads popped out of the water, looked at us menacingly, and grunted threateningly. We did not feel safe in the raft and Dr. Watson suggested that we paddle slowly to the river bank and wait there until the hippos got used to us and we could pass. We parked in the shade of a mangrove tree, hoping that the menacing grunts would stop. My friend remarked, "Here we are quite safe." He shouldn't have said that, because in that instant our raft was lifted up high. There had been a hippo under the water, and when she surfaced we found ourselves on top of her. Luckily, she was more surprised than we were. Our raft slid down her back, into the water, and the hippo swam quickly away. Later we lent the same raft to the Austrian consul. He was lucky, too. A bull hippo bit the raft in two but missed the consul, who was able to swim to safety.

One day when we tried to photograph a mother with her baby among a herd of females we witnessed the most amazing byplay. The mother had noticed us and was worried about her baby's safety. So she picked her up in her giant jaws, then turned around to hide her from us. Then the other hippos surrounded her, hiding mother and child from our view. In the meantime, the mother pushed her infant under the water. When the baby popped up, they immediately covered her. It was an organized effort to protect the baby from the evil eye of our camera. This experience again proved to me that we often falsely underestimate the intelligence of most creatures of the wild and overestimate our own.

The maternal instinct of the hippo was made manifest to me in a most dramatic and heartbreaking manner when I was directing an MGM film, *Zebra in the Kitchen*. For one sequence in the film, we needed a baby hippo and a full-grown mother hippo. It so happened that we owned a lovely baby hippo, but no large female. A circus passing through Los Angeles owned a big female, so I hired her for one day. She was delivered to our ranch in a large truck. As soon as we let the ramp down, the female ambled down to our shallow hippo pool and immediately adopted our baby, loving her, nuzzling her, and never letting her out of her sight. The needfulness of the baby was equally strong. She loved her foster mother and kept staying under her. The scene was finished in the afternoon, and the time had arrived to return the female to the circus, but the two hippos refused to leave each other's side. We tried to separate them with force, pushing long poles between them, but to no avail. The big female became furious, snapped the poles, and chased us away. This was the time when I jumped over a six-foot fence without any difficulty. (My previous high-jump record, in high school, had been five feet five inches.)

I telephoned the owner of the circus and offered to buy the female at a very high price. The answer was a definite no. The hippo was part of an act, and the circus was booked to be in Dallas in forty-eight hours, and he had to have his hippo back by nightfall. I was brokenhearted, and so was the baby. Finally we were forced to use a giant road grader to push the big, unhappy female up the ramp of the truck.

Although the members of a hippo herd stay very close to each other and seem to enjoy one another's company, fighting often breaks out among the three-ton bulls. They use their giant canines and incisors on each other, with the result that most bulls are scarred. The wounds heal amazingly fast and without infection because of an alkaline glandular discharge that oozes through the pores of the hippo's thick skin. This discharge is reddish, which led observers in the past to believe that hippos sweat blood.

My first encounter with hippos was at Lake Santa Lucia in Natal, one of the most beautiful wildlife areas in southern Africa. The lake connects with the Indian Ocean, and this is one of the few places where crocs and hippos meet sharks. I did not hear any adventurous encounters between sharks and crocodilians, but *The Guinness Book of Animal Facts and Feats* mentions that a hippo once destroyed a three-hundred-pound blue pointer shark in the surf. There, at the lake, full of flamingos, pelicans, and other colorful wildlife, I accompanied a game guard on a hippo tunnel patrol. The hippos create tunnels as they leave the lake and eat themselves through the heavy vegetation and tall reeds. The tunnels are used by poachers to kill hippos for their tusks, hides, and meat. The hunters often place snares inside these tunnels. Then when the hippo returns to the lake through the tunnel, the thin wire cuts through his neck and the hippo is condemned to a slow death in the cruel trap. The game guards on tunnel patrol search the waters for tunnels and then walk through them looking for snares. This is a very dangerous assignment. If a hippo by chance makes its return to the lake when the game guard is in the tunnel, and if the animal charges, there is nowhere to hide. Many brave game guards have lost their lives to hippos while trying to protect them. Luckily, when I participated in a tunnel patrol, hippos respected my American passport and my membership in the Explorers Club and so did not meet us head on in any of the tunnels we examined.

One animal I made friends with on the Nile was a bull hippo who had been banished from his herd by a stronger herd bull. One day, shortly after my arrival at Para Lodge, I was walking across a meadow toward our boat dock when, out of nowhere, a very large hippo appeared directly in front of me. Needless to say, I was somewhat anxious—in fact, my pulse rose to 120 from its usual 80. (You may find it odd, but it is my habit to take my pulse whenever I am scared.) Slowly and carefully I continued to move toward the river, never taking my eye off the hippo. I became even more nervous when the animal decided to follow me. But when we arrived at the bank of the Nile, he simply plopped into the water and went to sleep alongside the ferry landing. When no one else around me seemed to be concerned or curious, I asked who this hippo was. "Just one of the gang," came the reply. "His name's Henry."

Remember the buffalo that befriended the crocodile? Well, Henry had chosen the human companionship that was always available at the busy dock. He liked to sleep by our boat when we were anchored there, and our engine acted as his alarm clock. Sometimes, as on the day we first met, he would walk among the bungalows of the lodge, never bothering anybody. Pretty amazing for a wild creature.

When Ralph Helfer and I established Africa USA, we bought three young hippos and placed them in our lake. Strangely, two of the hippos ganged up against the third one, so we moved the underdog into another lake. While she was grazing around the lake our white donkey joined her. From then on the two animals were inseparable. When the little hippo was in the lake, the little donkey stayed close by the shore.

Soon Helfer realized that we had a trained hippo. When we led the donkey away, the hippo would climb out of the lake and follow the donkey. This gave us the idea of making the hippo a permanent character in our *Cowboy in Africa* television show. We called her Trashcan Annie because she ate everything in sight. Whenever we needed a shot of Trashcan Annie entering a house, all we had to do was take the donkey through the door and Trashcan Annie would follow him faithfully. In this way, we got most interesting scenes of a young hippo going to all the places where hippos usually do not go. Even the best animal trainers in Hollywood could not fully understand how we could train a hippo that well. We never gave away the secret that our white donkey was the trainer.

The most incredible story about a hippo was captured on film by a friend of mine whose pictures later appeared in *Life* magazine. While I was filming elephants, my friend Ruecastle was filming hippos at a water hole about a hundred miles south of my camp. There was a great drought at the time, and the water holes were very shallow. An impala approached and began to drink. Suddenly, a five-foot crocodile lunged at the impala, caught her, and pulled her into the water hole. A hippo saw this outrage and, to my friend's great surprise, she waded into the pool and stepped on the croc. In pain and surprise, the croc released the impala, which then staggered out of the water hole with her intestines hanging out of her torn belly. She collapsed about thirty feet from the water. Now the charitable hippo walked to the side of the injured creature and, with her giant mouth, tried to push the intestines back into the belly, where they belonged. It was the only recorded case of a hippo giving first aid to an injured impala. Unfortunately, the impala died within a few minutes, and the hippo had to give up her work as a Good Samaritan. The crocodile waited until the hippo had departed, then walked out of the water and pulled the dead impala back in the water hole. This short film by Mr. Ruecastle, a great African nature photographer, proved to animal behaviorists that animals have some unsuspected sides to their natures. It is not only man who has a soul.

8 Androcles and the Rhino

THERE ARE ONLY about eleven hundred white rhinos left in all of Africa, and I must mention with a dash of pride that I have met at least five hundred fifty of them. Most of them live in Zululand, in Natal, where I spent a great deal of time.

In the summer of 1963, I directed a film for MGM titled *Rhino*. Since there are no rhinos in Culver City, California, I had to travel eleven thousand miles to the place where rhinos are.

The rhinos could not find a nicer place to live than Zululand, with its rolling green hills, lovely mountains, the Umfolozi River, and Lake Santa Lucia, where millions of flamingos and thousands of hippos and crocodiles also make their home.

Our base of operation was at Mtubatuba. When I asked a Zulu why anyone would call a township Mtubatuba, he answered me with great clarity, "Mtubatuba in Zulu means 'The one who jumps and jumps.'" I still found it strange that a town should be named The-one-who-jumps-and-jumps, so I inquired further. Again, his answer was sensible. In this locality a Zulu chief was born and, since he was a giant of a baby, he did not come out easily from his mother's womb. The witch doctor, anxious to help the delivery, jumped up and down on the mother's belly. The jumping technique worked, and finally the mother delivered a healthy child who later became a big chief. Our base was called Mtubatuba in memory of the witch doctor who knew when, where, and how to jump.

But, getting back to rhinos, the white rhinos are not really white. It seems their original popular name was lost in translation. The Afrikaans word *wijde* (meaning "wide") was mistakenly changed to *white* in English. The official name for this species is the "square-lipped rhino"; and it is because of these wide lips that it was given the Afrikaans nickname that has now become the English misnomer. Black rhinos, which are black only when they wallow in black mud, are much smaller. The white rhino is the heaviest land mammal next to the African elephant. He may weigh as much as seven thousand pounds. And I, who was chased by a big one, must testify that the awkward-looking primeval creature is as nimble on its feet as a ballerina and as fast as a locomotive. Luckily, white rhinos are good-natured creatures compared to black rhinos. This makes it easy for the tourist, for the situation is not unlike the old Westerns, where the villains are identified by their black hats, and the good guys by their white ones. It is wise to avoid

Zululand rhinos on the run

the villainous black rhino, but one need not have too much fear of the giant white rhino.

Rhinos have remained very much the same over the past ten million years. This could mean that they are perfectly evolved. But they were perfect only until men invented firearms and discovered Africa, and until some Chinese decided that powdered rhino horn was a powerful aphrodisiac. This is not true, but believing it must have given some psychological satisfaction to the Chinese. Many white settlers killed the rhinos out of cruelty, simply because the large beasts were an easy target. At the same time, poachers killed them to sell their horns to the Chinese. For these reasons, by the turn of this century, the number of majestic white rhinos had been reduced to about twenty. At this point, some conservationists decided to stop the slaughter and save the rhino. From then on, dedicated game guards fought ferocious battles with poachers. I witnessed some of these encounters, and, under the leadership of Ian Player (elder brother of the famous golfer Gary Player), the rhino's battle was won. The end result is that, at least for the present, white rhinos are not endangered.

I decided to make a film, in a dramatic but documentary style, about this heroic effort, and so I followed the activities of Ian Player and his game guards. The first time I was charged by a rhino was when Ian Player had tranquilized a huge female with his hypodermic rifle. This rhino had wandered off the reservation and was thus exposed to poachers. Player's objective was to catch her ladyship and transport her back to Umfolozi, where she would be safe. I tried to film the whole procedure. The rhino was darted and captured. She soon fell asleep under the influence of the anaesthetic. Then Player tried a new antidote, which he thought would take at least five minutes to put the giant creature on her feet again. He was wrong. The antidote took effect immediately and the rhino was on her feet in thirty seconds and I, standing in front of her, was her immediate target.

My photographer, whose camera was running, got on film the

Mack Sennett scene of the year: The drugged rhino running, the MGM crew running faster, and me running the fastest because I was the closest to the deadly horns. I could feel the breath of the monster on my neck when Ian Player ran up close to the rhino's ear and shouted in Zulu. I don't know what he said, as I don't speak Zulu, but the rhino stopped. When Ian yelled, she stopped in her tracks, and I took the opportunity to disappear into a ditch behind a thorn tree. Later I learned that rhinos have abominable eyesight, but very acute hearing, and a shout in the ear sounds to them like a fired shot. But from that frightful moment on, I formed a new habit. I avoided standing in front of sleeping rhinos, but if I did, I made sure that Player was present.

Soon after, a game guard reported that a black rhino was dying in a poacher's snare. I drove with Player and Harry Guardino, the American actor, to see whether we could ease the

The rhino that attacked Ivan Tors being tranquilized by Ian Player and Harry Guardino

pain of this dying rhino. It was a horrible sight. A poacher had placed a wire snare square on a bush. As the black rhino was browsing he stuck his giant head between the loop of the wire snare prepared in the shape of a lasso. As he tried to disentangle himself, he pulled the wire noose tighter and tighter until the wire cut into his flesh at least one inch deep around his neck. With each movement the cut deepened and in a few minutes the poor rhino could have severed all the arteries of his neck. It was a cruel sight. Player acted immediately. He shot a strong dose of painkiller into the suffering animal and as soon as the rhino stopped struggling, we cut off the wire. The damage to the neck was horrendous. It did not seem as if we could help this miserable monster. But Player was determined, and with the help of eighty strong Zulus and a winch, we loaded the sick animal onto a giant van and took him to our main compound, where we installed him in a fortified enclosure. There we filled him with antibiotics and treated the wound with sulfa powder.

The Zulus, who give names to everybody, named the rhino Guardino. For three weeks, we treated him with more shots and administered sulfa daily. It wasn't an easy task. The rhino fought us "horn and hoof," but after ten days, as the wound slowly healed, the black rhino realized that we were his friends. He stopped his fitful threatenings and began to take lucerne and hay out of our hands. In three weeks, the healing was complete. In six weeks Guardino (the rhino, not the actor) was allowed to return to the wild. I guess it was the first time in history the so-called vicious black rhino was used to prove that love conquers all. And even today in the Umkuzi Game Reserve, where we relocated the rhino, game guards can walk up to this feared beast and tickle him under the chin. A rhino named Guardino is still grateful to man.

Living in Zululand, I learned that all the Olympic high-jump records are underachievements. There is a tree in Umfolozi where one of the branches is marked at a height of twelve feet. This is how high a game guard jumped when chased by a rhino. All Olympic athletes could shatter records if rhinos were to chase them around the track.

Rhinos are territorial, meaning that the strongest male with his selected harem will occupy the land with the tastiest vegetation and the best water supply. He will mark his boundaries with his urine and chase away every other rhino, unless it happens to be an attractive female. I had an excellent chance to study the meaning of rhino territoriality when two of my friends, John Seago and Tony Parkinson, received a government contract to relocate all the black rhinos from the Isiolo district to different game reserves. The reason was that the land-starved Turkana wished to settle in this wild area. The task of capturing hundreds of uncooperative black rhinos in a large, rocky, mountainous area seemed to me at that time a back-breaking impossibility. Strangely, I was wrong. The territoriality of the rhino made it much easier than anticipated. On the first day, Tony Parkinson, a skilled flier, spotted the first herd in the bottom land, where the bushes were the greenest and the water was fresh. A rhino family was captured that very day without much difficulty because Land-Rovers and pursuing trucks could operate in this flat area.

Next time when Tony took off to locate a second herd, he spotted another herd, to his great surprise, exactly where the first herd had been, in the bottom land. Animal nature is opportunistic, and the second strongest male had moved immediately into the vacated territory, where food was the best and the water the sweetest. After the second group was captured and translocated, the pattern repeated itself. Another rhino family moved down from the rocky area to occupy the best neighborhood. To catch all the rhinos they had to translocate, John and Tony could stay put in the same comfortable area without being forced to climb rugged mountains with their Land-Rovers and capture vehicles.

John Seago, who was a slight, elderly British gentleman, looked like anything but a trapper. He had the appearance of a minister or a barrister. He told a most interesting life story. Serving in the British Navy in World War II and exposed to the icy winds of the North Sea, he developed a very serious case of tuberculosis. He was skin and bones, so seriously ill that he was told that he lived on borrowed time. In desperation, he moved to Kenya and tried his luck as a trapper. In the healthy climate of the Kenyan highlands, he was completely cured. Life in nature made him strong and tough, although he never put on weight. None of us who were younger could outwalk him or outlast him in the bush. Still, he had never lost his impeccable British manners. He carried himself as a gentleman amid the most primitive conditions and among the most primitive people. When he served tea in an old tent, the china and tea were the finest. His considerate, polite nature never faltered, even in the midst of the greatest dangers.

We were together again in the Northern Frontier District of Kenya, where I was filming a picture called *Cowboy in Africa*. For one of the scenes, we needed a vicious black rhino. I hired John Seago to make the capture. We spotted an angry bull with a daggerlike horn, and Tony shot him in the buttock with our hypodermic gun. But the needle did not penetrate the tough muscle and the rhino turned furiously and charged John. The long horn hooked him under the crotch and threw him a good ten feet up in the air. As the little Englishman was catapulting over us, and as we watched in horror, he screamed down, "Don't worry, chappies. I'm all right." I couldn't help laughing. Even when thrown by a rhino and in deadly danger, he was more worried about *our* being worried than about himself.

This rhino kept giving us trouble. When we finally captured the bull and caged him, the crazy ill-tempered beast attacked his own cage viciously and broke off his horn. This was another blow. On film, a rhino without a horn would look, not like a rhino, but more like a five-thousand-pound pig. What to do? Again we tranquilized the rhino. Our ingenious makeup man created a great-looking horn from hard rubber, and we attached this with rubber cement to the nose of our sleeping beauty. When he woke up, he had a mighty horn again, and I could finish the sequence. The legend of the rubber horn spread fast via bush telegraphy. In the frontier district, they are still talking about the rhino with a rubber horn.

Interestingly, a rhino's horn is not a horn at all. It is actually made of matted hair that is so hard that it can puncture a two-by-four or impale a human. Sawing off a rhino horn will cause only temporary damage, because the horn will eventually grow back. The growth rate is estimated at two inches per year.

Another distinctive characteristic is that white rhinos are the only mammals that cannot swim. For this reason, even experienced naturalists may misunderstand when they see a drowning rhino. They assume that a crocodile has dragged the rhino under the water. No crocodile has the strength to drown a rhino, but often a rhino will try to ford a river, and when he loses the land under his feet, he cannot recover.

Trevor Howard told me an unusual story that happened when he and his wife, Helen, spent a night at Treetops. Treetops is a small hotel built on high stilts opposite a water hole in the Aberdare Mountains of Kenya. Queen Elizabeth and Prince Philip spent their honeymoon there. It is an excellent observation point for studying wildlife at night. Most animals come to the water hole unperturbed by the strong reflectors that light up the area. The night when Trevor and Helen were there, a rhino came with her calf to the water hole to drink. The rhino baby suddenly got into deep trouble and started to sink into the soft mud. There was nothing the mother could do to save her child from drowning. Suddenly, a female elephant, who was nearby, intervened. Extending her six-foot trunk, she reached out to the little rhino and, using her great strength, pulled the baby back to safety. She did not expect gratitude, and she did not get any. The mother rhino charged the humanitarian elephant, nearly killing her. Maternal instinct told the rhino only one thing: "Somebody is touching my baby." That shows why elephants are famous for their wisdom, while rhinos are renowned for their small brains.

It was interesting to observe how maternal instincts determine distinctive patterns of behavior. The white rhinos, who graze in the open savanna, have their young always in front of them, because predators in the savanna always attack from behind. In this way, the mother can serve as bulwark between the baby and an aggressive hungry lion. The black rhinos, on the other hand, browse in bush country. They, in turn, keep their young behind them. Thus, if they happen to flush a sleeping predator out of the bushes, the mother, not the baby, would become the primary target.

So it won't seem that rhinos exist only to protect their own interests, I must point out that the presence of the rhino in Africa is important to the survival of smaller animals. When it rains, rhinos like to wallow in the mud, and by their sheer weight they form an indentation a few feet deep that will fill up with water. When the rain has stopped, a water hole will have been created for smaller creatures who cannot carve out their own water tank. Nothing is useless in nature. Each creature has its job cut out, and the rhino is no exception.

The rhinos' only living enemies are poachers. Elephants won't bother them, and other animals would not dare. I have heard of only one exception. One night in the Ngorongoro Crater, a rhino that had lived in peace with a neighborhood pride of lions was attacked by the whole pride and cruelly killed. No one knows what triggered the attack. There was plenty of food around for the lions. The crater was teeming with prey, and it is certainly easier to kill a zebra than a rhino. Perhaps the lions were simply testing their own strength, as they often do by attacking bull buffaloes (when they often get gored and come out second best).

The first rhino I ever encountered in Africa was a famous old lady. Her name was Gertie, and she lived at the Amboseli Game Reserve at the foot of Kilimanjaro. She was the most photographed rhino in the area. Gertie had no earlobes — a genetic failure — and her horn looked like a seven-foot spear. Although she was protected, she was killed by a poacher one night, and her monumental horn was cut off to end up somewhere in Hong Kong.

The film *Rhino* was a turning point in my life because I fell in love with Africa and African wildlife as a result. Since then, I have visited Africa nearly every year and often three or four times a year. One person who taught me an invaluable amount about the animals and ecology of the area was Makubu, the guide assigned to me by Ian Player. He was a dignified Zulu elder, the sergeant of the Zulu game guards, and although he was in his sixties, I could hardly keep up with him as we walked the African bush together. Makubu was like a real Dr. Dolittle — he could talk to the animals. When we needed a female rhino, he imitated the call of the male rhino and a female would come. When we needed a male rhino, he imitated the mating call of a female rhino and a male would turn up. He could call zebras, wildebeests, or any other animal. It was sheer magic.

His greatest act was to imitate the song of the honey guide, which is a beautiful African bird that loves to eat the larvae of the wild honey bee. Since its beak is not strong enough to break open the honeycomb, the honey guide, in a miraculous scheme of nature's, forms a partnership with a ferocious little animal known as the honey badger, or ratel. When the honey guide locates a beehive, it sings a song that the honey badger recognizes. The honey badger hightails it to the place where the honey guide's song is coming from, climbs the tree, and with his strong claws, tears the beehive apart. Then, while the badger feeds on honey, the honey guide feeds on larvae. This is one of the best partnerships in nature. Makubu learned the song of the honey guide, and now he, too, could call the honey badger.

Once we were fording a river. Makubu stopped me and

pointed to a baboon that was drinking on the river bank. He explained that if a baboon puts its mouth to the water, there is no danger of crocodiles. But if a baboon rapidly scoops the water toward his mouth with his hand, then crocodiles are around. It was a good fact to know.

What Makubu taught me, I taught my sons. Their lessons in acting quickly and calmly started early. When they were old enough to go on a field trip, we made our first stop in Zululand. I chartered a small plane with a pilot to fly us from Kenya to Mtubatuba. On our way back, my youngest son sat next to the pilot, my other two sons sat in the next two seats, and I occupied the last seat, next to the small cargo space facing the cargo hatch. We took off from a grass strip, and when we were cruising at nine thousand feet, I fell asleep in my seat. In my sleep, I somehow kicked out the cargo hatch and I fell halfway out of the plane before I caught something I could hang onto for dear life. The balance of the Beechcraft was upset as I hung outside, but the open hatch acted as an air break. Luckily, with the help of my sons, I was pulled back into the plane. We could not, however, close the open hatch. The skilled pilot landed the plane on an open field and, after fixing the cargo hatch, we took off again. (Since then, when I am in a plane, even on the ground, I fasten my seat belt.) So you see, there are many reasons why I shall never forget Zululand.

My adventures with rhinos did not end in Zululand. After returning to California, I purchased two young rhinos from the Umfolozi Game Reserve, where they had a sudden surplus and not enough grazing ground. We transferred the two white rhinos to Soledad Canyon where our TV show *Daktari* was being produced. At that time I was the first private person in the United States in possession of such treasures.

The two young giants were tamed very fast. All animals are survival-oriented, and these rhinos soon realized that, far from being a threat, we were the benevolent suppliers of lucerne and water. Our presence no longer made them nervous. On the contrary, when I began to play "oxpeckers" with them, our relationship even became affectionate. I had noticed in the wild that oxpeckers, attractive small African birds with red beaks, have a symbiotic relationship with elephants, buffaloes, rhinos, large antelopes, and even warthogs. These clever birds land on the wild creatures and feed on the ticks and other parasites that pester the animals. They even work on the earlobes and inside the nostrils. It creates a soothing feeling for the beasts to be liberated from the irritants, and they enjoy the attentions of the oxpeckers. As an experiment, I started to pick the skin of our rhinos, first with a long wooden stick, then later with my hand. The rhinos appreciated this activity, and soon we were more than good friends. My associates and I were allowed to sit on their backs and massage them. This was a part of the philosophy we called "affection training." And I became the first human oxpecker.

Unfortunately, the male rhino did not survive the first winter. Our female rhino became a young widow and very, very lonesome. As we could not obtain another male rhino on short notice, Ralph Helfer suggested that we try a zoological first and let our bull water buffalo, who was a widower, join the female rhino in her ample enclosure. I accepted the suggestion, and Ralph became the marriage broker between rhino and water buffalo. The relationship was very successful. The two large animals became inseparable, even though the marriage was not consummated.

It has been proved to me again and again that animals are just as needful of companionship as humans are, and the nearness of another creature is a psychological imperative. Later we tried to join other individuals of different species. At our ranch, a Rhodesian ridgeback dog and a young lion formed a most affectionate relationship. It was interesting to see that even when the female lion had grown to five times the size of the male dog, she still deferred to the male and ate only after the dog had finished his meal.

*

In Namibia, on our game farm, we have four friendly white rhinos grazing around the house. They are not tame. We do not want them to become tame, for they have to survive in the wild; but they are accustomed to us. They know by now that they are not threatened. The grass is greenest around the house, and that is where they like to graze. Their aggressive instincts have subsided completely. We are as used to them as to the cows that supply our milk, and in fact, the cows and the four rhinos often graze together.

When I visited Zululand some twenty years ago, there were no white rhinos anywhere except on the Umfolozi Game Reserve. It was Ian Player's wisdom to scatter the surplus all over Africa and thus to establish breeding herds on other reservations. His great fear at that time was that an epidemic of anthrax or a similar disease would wipe out all the white rhinos of Umfolozi, and such a disaster would spell the end for this most ancient and interesting beast. Now the future of the white rhino is assured. There are small herds now even in Texas and New York State. I am grateful to Ian Player. It would be a sad world if there were no rhinos, elephants, whales, or giraffes. I certainly would not like to live in such a world.

9 Yapee

ONE EASTER SUNDAY I called my son in Africa, and when I asked him how he was, his answer shocked me. "I had to shoot Yapee," he said, with sorrow in his voice. I did not want to believe what I just heard. Yapee was the pet baboon we were all crazy about. He liked to ride on motorcycles, sitting on the back, holding onto the rider. He was one smart baboon but his genetic characteristics sealed his fate. He was an alpha or dominant, baboon.

It is my belief that baboons are closest to man in behavior patterns. They are well organized and they live in a hierarchical society, in a way our ancestors lived at the time when they were hunter-gatherers.

Like men, baboons are excellent survivors. They can adapt easily to new conditions, but, of course, they are guided by certain genetic characteristics. They have a pecking order like that of hens and cocks in a barnyard. The boss is the alpha baboon. He is the emperor, and though he will have other aggressive males around him, all these will act subserviently toward him. They will behave aggressively toward each other only until the rank order is established, but after that there will be a number one baboon, number two, three, and so on.

Yapee was a tiny orphan when Jan Oelofse found him. He had probably fallen out of a tree and was injured. The baboon

Yapee

troop must have been frightened by something like a gunshot and left the tiny one behind. Jan picked him up, took him home, and nursed him back to health. This is how Yapee became a family pet. He was attached to a fifty-foot-long light chain that was tied to a twenty-foot-high pole, and Jan had placed a two-by-four on the top of the pole. At night, Yapee would climb the pole and sleep on the top, where he was safe from leopards—night hunters who love to eat baboons. By the time I met Yapee, he had passed the age of puberty and was already a giant. Because of his size, strength, and threatening giant canines, he would probably have been the leader of his troop, if he had had one.

But he accepted a man as his boss and acted affectionately to all of us when we approached him singly.

Every morning after I had had my coffee, I visited Yapee. He would immediately embrace me. He had a wide grin, and he chattered his teeth in a funny way as an expression of pleasure and joy. Then I would start to groom his fur, since monkeys and apes are always grooming each other, and Yapee would groom my hair at the same time. Once, he tried to have sex with my leg, but when I told him no, he stopped. When I brought him a female in heat, he was uninterested. Yapee had been exposed to humans only, and he believed that he was a part of the human race.

I studied Yapee all the time. He was extremely intelligent. Once I saw him lying on the ground and, because the small of his back was itching, he tried to scratch it, but he could not reach the spot. He looked around and broke off a branch from a nearby bush and stripped off all the leaves. Now he had a long stick. He looked at the stick in his hand, then broke off a large piece. The stick was then exactly long enough to reach the itch, and Yapee began to scratch his back. He had constructed a back scratcher. This made him a toolmaker, an identity that formerly was supposed to distinguish men from animals. Another time, I observed him when he wanted something that was out of his reach. Again he used a branch as a rake and raked it close enough to have it within his grasp.

One day we had a bad storm, and the pole to which he was tied snapped off at about four feet. The break was quite clean and almost flat. The two-by-four that he used as his perch had broken off as well. Yapee picked up the two-by-four and attempted to reconstruct the perch. He placed the wooden bar on the top of what now was only a four-foot pole. Of course it fell off. He tried to balance it, but it would not balance. Suddenly Yapee centered it properly, jumped on top of it, and kept it balanced by shifting his weight. Yapee had both a new game and the satisfaction of reconstructing his perch.

The trouble with Yapee started when an outsider saw us playing with him. Any visitor, seeing the friendly baboon playing with me or Jan or my boys, believed that this was a safe baboon. He was far from safe. When a second human approached Yapee, he immediately turned on that person. This was because, according to baboon genetics, he believed that he was number two. When a number three approached, he had to savage that number three in order to put him in his place and teach him that he was subservient to Yapee. Members of our household knew this, and we approached Yapee only one at a time. But visitors or young children around the farm did not know this, and so a few of them were chased and bitten.

Tragedy struck when George, one of our workers, asked my son Steve, who was playing with Yapee at the time, to take his picture with Yapee. Steve stepped back, took the camera from George, and George stepped next to Yapee. But Steve was still too close, and Yapee's alpha baboon instinct reasoned that George was an intruding number three who had to be dealt with severely. Instantly, Yapee attacked George. By the time Steve succeeded in restraining the wild baboon, George was minus part of his scalp. This was the first serious offense.

While I was away from Africa, things became worse. More visitors made mistakes, more of them were attacked, and a native child was nearly killed. So when Yapee broke his chain and took off toward the servants' quarters, Jan gave the order: "Steve, shoot him, or he'll kill one of the children."

Steve was number two to Jan, and he instinctively obeyed his number one's order. He aimed and pulled the trigger. Yapee was hit in a vital spot. He turned around and looked at Steve in disbelief. It was a look that Steve will never forget. It made him think of Caesar when Brutus stabbed him. Yapee touched the spot where the bullet hit him, then collapsed dead.

I was stunned when I heard the story, for I was about to return to the farm to study Yapee further. I knew that he had had to be killed, but I felt that we had lost one of the family. We preserved his skull, an extremely large one with space for a fairly large brain.

My first acquaintance with a baboon came about in Johannesburg when I was preparing to film *Rhino*. Someone told me that the animal shelter had a fairly tame baboon that they would love to get rid of and perhaps I might be able to use him in the film. Sven Persson, my cameraman, drove me to the shelter, and I was introduced to a young baboon named Jackie. Jackie and I became fast friends. I carried him on my shoulder and fed him choice morsels, mostly fruit, which he loved. I was unfamiliar with baboons then, my first time in Africa, but I noticed a few important characteristics. One was their tendency to cling to each other. In this case, Jackie clung to me. Hysteria was another. Whenever something scared Jackie — whether animal, human, or anything noisy — he instinctively bit me. A small baboon has no other defense than biting, and in his fear, he did not differentiate between friend and foe. For this reason, I stopped carrying Jackie on my shoulder. I tied him to my hut.

In preparing a film sequence on the immobilization of wildlife, Dr. Keith Ditman, a psycho-pharmacologist, who was my technical consultant, wished to observe the effect of Valium on Jackie. He peeled a banana, stuck the capsule of Valium in the fruit, and then handed the banana to Jackie. Jackie loved bananas, as all primates do. To our great surprise, he did not eat the banana at first. He broke it open where the capsule was hidden, took out the capsule, looked at it, and swallowed it. Then he ate the banana and looked at us victoriously. His expression meant, "You dummies. You think you can fool a baboon. If you want me to swallow a capsule, just tell me. You really underestimate me." We looked dumbfounded at Jackie, having learned never to belittle the intelligence of a baboon.

Dr. Felix Rodriguez De La Fuente, the Spanish ethologist, calls baboons the inheritors of the earth. I tend to agree with him. If the human race destroys itself foolishly, baboons are the most likely, among all primates, to take man's place.

The Guinness Book of Animal Facts and Feats states that the most intelligent monkeys are baboons. According to the book, the most famous example was a male chacma baboon called Jack, who used to work the railway signals at Uitenhage Station, about two hundred miles north of Port Elizabeth, in South Africa. The story goes that a railwayman named Wylde lost both his legs below the calf as the result of an accident on the Port Elizabeth main line in 1877, and so he was given a job as a signalman at Uitenhage Station. In order to make the journey between his wooden shack and the signal box, a distance of some hundred fifty yards, he constructed a trolley in which he could propel himself along the track with the aid of a pole. One day he saw Jack for sale in the local market and purchased him as a pet. The baboon soon became extremely devoted to his master, and during the next few months, Wylde trained him to fetch water, sweep out the shack, and even to hand a special key to passing engine drivers, who used it to adjust switches farther up the line. The baboon also learned to push his master in the trolley to the signal box, where the animal would then sit and watch with great interest as the signalman pulled the levers.

Soon Jack was able to operate the signals for the Graaf Reinet and Port Elizabeth trains while Wylde sat on the trolley ready to correct any mistakes he might make. Eventually, however, the baboon became so proficient at his job that he was able to carry out the whole operation by himself while his master remained in the shack. He was never known to make a mistake. This amazing partnership lasted for over nine years, until Jack died from tuberculosis in 1890.

At the time of this writing, another chacma baboon, Jock, is working as a signalman on a branch line near Pretoria, South Africa. Unlike Jack, however, this baboon is paid 1s. 6d. a day and gets a bottle of beer every Saturday night!

Although many of the apes, especially the orangutans, look more human than baboons, the social structure of the baboons is closer to ours. First of all, baboons, like early humans, left the dense forests and moved onto the savannas. They organized much larger tribes than the apes, finding safety in numbers. Their body size is closer to the size of the original humans. They feed on grass seeds mainly, but they will eat almost everything: berries, tubers, scorpions (after skillfully removing the stinger), termites, field mice, and even small antelopes. So we must call them omnivores, as humans are called. On the grassland they have to be well organized and post sentries to protect themselves from such predators as lions, leopards, hyenas, and jackals. Just as humans withdraw at night — originally into caves, later into tents, huts, or houses — baboons, afraid of the dark, climb trees to spend the night in considerable safety.

Their care for the young is exemplary, and this is one of the main reasons why they are such good survivors. The baby baboon is born after a gestation period of five and a half months. The newborn looks like a scrawny little human, almost entirely black. Zoologists believe the black color triggers protective feelings in the elders, attracting them to the infant. For about six months, the baby never leaves the mother in order to be close to the milk supply. For the first two months, the infant clings to the mother's belly, but as it grows older, it changes positions. Soon, the funny little toylike creature, with its enormous ears and pink buttocks, will cling to the mother's rump, holding onto the mother's tail. Next, the infant will ride on the mother's back, jockey-style. This is the "easy rider" stage. While the mother carries the baby, she is constantly feeding. Finally, after five or six months, the baby will jump off occasionally and imitate the mother, pulling out grass and tasting the seeds. This is the time for it to meet other babies, and they play and gambol together, but always under the careful watch of a number of adults. The young ones are handled gently by all adults, and the males often carry the babies. The giant alpha baboon always watches the group activity. His duty is to lead and defend. Being close to their mothers and other adults who are protective gives an unusual security to young baboons, which unquestionably contributes to the strength, determination, and hardiness of the species.

The next step in the life of the young involves exploration and engaging in young baboon exercises, all designed to improve their agility and skill at climbing. The most important lifesaver for a baboon will be a nearby tree to facilitate a fast getaway if danger approaches in the form of a leopard, hyena, or python.

There are incredible legends about the self sacrifice and cooperation of baboons. Stories are told about a leopard attacking a troop of baboons and five elders jumping on the leopard. By the time the leopard had killed two of them, the other three have succeeded in biting through the leopard's jugular vein with their enormous male canines and have killed the enemy.

An African hunter told the following story. He was asleep in his sleeping bag at night when he heard some commotion. Opening his eyes, he realized that he was surrounded by a large troop of baboons. Being an experienced man, he remained still but kept a finger on the trigger of his gun. Then the baboons slowly moved to either side of him, creating a path and indicating that he should follow them. He was puzzled and scared but went with the baboons. They guided him to a spot where a baby baboon was lying on the ground, dying. From the color of the vomit, the hunter recognized that the infant had swallowed some kind of poison. He picked it up and forced water from his canteen into its mouth. The baboon then vomited, and more and more of the poison came out. Eventually the vomit lacked the color of the poison, and the baby, although absolutely exhausted, showed the awakening of certain vital signs that had been absent before. Soon the little baboon got up and joined the others. While the treatment was taking place, the hunter had been surrounded by a circle of big males. When the baby revived, the circle opened and the man was allowed to walk back to his sleeping bag. There were no witnesses, so we must take the hunter's word for it. After studying baboons, I think the story is credible.

Observing baboon behavior in the wild is not easy. Baboons are wary of humans and avoid us. Jane Goodall was patient enough to be accepted by a troop, and she made a magnificent film in Tanzania. In Kenya, the University of California at Berkeley supports a research station in Gilgil, in the Great Rift Valley, where we were permitted to observe and photograph baboon behavior. The territory of this troop was an old cattle ranch where the cattle had pretty well destroyed the high grass. Thus, we could approach the baboons up close with our Volkswagen bus and then photograph scenes showing the baboons' interaction, breeding habits, and social structure. Most interesting to observe was the dominant baboon, the overlord who supervises and disciplines his troop. He himself very seldom engages in a fight. If a male from another troop intrudes on his territory, he will, with a raise of his eyebrow, instruct his underling males to attack and chase away the challenger. We soon realized that specific signals encourage the smaller, lesser males in their fight against an intruder who dares to challenge the superiority of their overlord. These signals indicate to them that, "if you are in trouble, I'll come to your aid. I'll finish off the bastard." With this backing, the smaller males often come out victorious against a larger intruder.

When the females are in heat, their genital area changes from a rosy color to cardinal red. Baboons are promiscuous and all the males are allowed to mount the receptive female, but the female can conceive only when the genital organs are bright red. At this time, the overlord will assert his rights, take the female aside, and copulate with her exclusively. In this system, all the males can have their pleasure, but the best seed will father the newborn, thus maintaining a strong genetic pool.

The ordering of rank among males begins when the young are between nine and eighteen months old. During this time, it is determined which ones are stronger, which have more courage, and which are timid. This is the most important period of infant development. Since it determines who will be the overlord, who the courtier, who the obedient bodyguard. Lately we have found that it is not physical strength that determines leadership in the pecking order, but a greater amount of testesterone, the male hormone, in the blood.

In Gilgil we tested the overlord. We threw out a big bunch of bananas to the troop. Before others could touch any of it, the boss baboon took full possession and refused to share with any of his constituents. Then he started to eat, keeping his eye on everyone. He allowed his second in command alone to steal away one fruit. Then he ate and ate until he fell over and went to sleep. Once the others were sure that the absolute monarch was harmless, they stole the rest of the bananas and finished them fast. It was then that I realized that baboon societies are not democracies but semibenevolent dictatorships.

As a result of their organized society, care for the young, defense of each other, and keeping safe at night, baboons have survived better than any other primate society. Today, baboons can be found all over Africa. Sometimes they are pests. Once, in the Masai Mara Game Reserve, my tent was pitched under a very large tree with baboons in it. The baboons amused themselves by throwing twigs on my head whenever I left my tent. In zoos they like to throw their dry feces at the onlookers. It amuses them to see how people scamper. Humor is an essential mark of civilization. Perhaps Dr. De La Fuente is right — after humans muff their chances, baboons will inherit the earth.

10   How to Love a Snake

IT MAY SOUND STRANGE, but in my family, everyone likes snakes. My children always wanted snakes for their birthdays and my wife complied with their wishes. Peter, at the age of five, was the proud owner of a boa constrictor and a tarantula, which he tried to tame. (Unfortunately, the tarantula committed suicide by jumping out of a second-story window and landing on the concrete in front of our garage.) Since snakes enjoy body heat, it was not unusual for me to be found reading a book in the garden with my shirt off and a boa constrictor wound around my chest.

I lost my fear of snakes in the Sierra Madre, in Mexico, when, looking up into the sky to admire an eagle, I inadvertently stepped on a rattlesnake nest. The intense rattling quickly made me focus on the ground instead of the sky. I stood motionless, staring at six fat rattlesnakes in threatening postures. They rattled, but did not strike. My playing statue for a few minutes settled them down; then I retraced my steps backward and got out of their circle. From this incident I had a strange spiritual sensation. Nature has endowed these creatures with an alarm system, and it was this that had stopped me from stepping on them, and thus I avoided being bitten. I was afraid of snakes no longer.

While I was producing *Sea Hunt,* my office was at the Eagle

Lion Studios on Santa Monica Boulevard. One day my friend Ralph Helfer (at that time a young animal dealer) stopped by my office and pulled a beautiful indigo snake out of his shirt and handed it to me. He told me that, since he had a few errands to do in the studio, he would like me to "snake sit" until he returned. "No sweat," I said, and took the snake from him. I pushed the snake's head under my shirt and the snake wound itself immediately around me in a comfortable position. Of course, he was invisible under my shirt. When Ralph left my office, I buzzed my secretary to tell her I was ready to give dictation. She came in with her shorthand book, sat down facing me, and I began to dictate.

In a few minutes, the snake became restless and started moving about under my shirt, tickling me. I nonchalantly reached in and pulled out the snake. My secretary was not prepared for this. She fainted dead away. I had to carry her to the couch and douse her with cold water. When she opened her eyes and saw the snake in my hand, she was about to faint again. I explained to her that the snake did not appear from inside my body and that I held this snake only for safekeeping until Helfer's return. The next day she started to look for another job.

While shooting *Daktari,* I received a call from New York from the producer of the Johnny Carson show. Johnny needed a guest for the following evening and he wanted me. The appearance would be important for me because *Daktari* had just begun its life on the airwaves, and the publicity would be very good for the show. Johnny Carson made one condition to the invitation. I must bring one of my pet animals, such as Clarence the Cross-Eyed Lion or Samson, my pet tiger. I called Ralph Helfer at the ranch and told him that I was taking the first plane in the morning and I wanted to ship one of our big cats to New York as well. He told me that was impossible because I would need health certificates and medical exams for interstate travel, and it would take at least three days to get the necessary documents ready. Then Ralph hit on an idea.

Ivan Tors and a 10-foot boa constrictor

"Why don't you take one of our big snakes? You can put it in a carry-on bag and keep the bag at your feet. Nobody would know that you are traveling with a thirteen-foot boa constrictor!" I accepted his suggestion.

The next morning, I carried a huge boa constrictor aboard the plane. The snake accepted the bag as a comfortable nest, and it was very unlikely that he would want to leave the nest for any reason. As soon as the jet had taken off, I opened the zipper of the bag so that my snake could have enough air. In the darkness, under my feet, rested my strange traveling companion. In front of me sat a very bald gentleman who acted very busy, adding up column after column of figures. He looked like an accountant working on tax returns. Finally, he got tired of his work, and with his right hand he took off his horn-rimmed glasses. He stretched and yawned, lifted his right arm over his seat, and dropped his glasses into my luggage, right on top of my boa constrictor. Before I could do anything, I saw his arm searching and probing behind him for the glasses. The snake was not bothered at all by the glasses resting on his head. Suddenly, the man touched the frame of his spectacles, pulled them up, and put them back on his nose. It was an exciting, suspenseful minute. This gentleman will never know where his glasses were, and how close he was to being bitten by the three hundred teeth of a boa constrictor. I pulled the zipper tighter, leaving an open space just large enough to let my snake have a little air. I realized how close *I* was to being banished forever from traveling on TWA.

Arriving in New York, I found a young publicist from MGM waiting for me with a limousine. We drove to midtown Manhattan to check into the Americana Hotel, which was only a short block away from the NBC building. Upon my arrival, I went into the bathroom, took the boa constrictor out of my luggage, and placed him in the bathtub. I checked around to make sure that there was no way for the snake to escape from the windowless bathroom. I closed the bathroom door and placed a DO NOT DISTURB sign on the doorknob. Then my companion and I took the elevator to the restaurant to have a bite before my television appearance. Forty-five minutes later, we were back in my suite.

I changed my clothes to get ready for *The Tonight Show* and entered the bathroom to pick up the snake. The snake was not in the bathroom. I couldn't imagine where it had gone. The snake was much too big around to disappear into the toilet bowl. There was no window. There was nowhere to hide. I lay down on the bathroom floor and searched for any possible way the snake could have disappeared. Then, under the sink, I discovered the snake in a dark coil around the hot water pipe. The steel-black skin just blended in with the black pipe, and the coil looked as if it were part of the sink. He was very, very comfortable. It took me and the publicist a good half hour to unwind the snake so I could place him in the bag and go off to NBC.

When I walked onto the stage, I had the big snake coiled around my body. My arms were high above my head, and the snake's head rested on my shoulder. I explained that I was not in danger because I did not present any threat to the snake. I was a tree to him; my raised arms were the branches. It was a safe place for a snake to be. Johnny Carson imitated my posture. "You mean, I look like a tree?" he asked. The boa immediately moved off of me and wound onto Johnny, who was a more handsome tree. To my great surprise, Johnny did not lose his nerve. He allowed the snake to climb onto him and find a comfortable position. He received tremendous applause from the audience as well as my respect.

Many tourists visiting Africa have a great fear of snakes. I always try to put their minds at ease. On my first expedition in Africa, I did not see a single snake in the wild. It was winter and all snakes were hibernating. When a few Zulu workers began to dig the foundation for a cook tent, they dug up four deadly snakes — a Gaboon viper, two puff adders, and a spitting cobra. Since they were hibernating and their metabolism was minimal, they were helpless. We placed the four snakes in a sack. We put the sack in the desk of our MGM accountant, Wendell Baggett. It took him some time to accept the four deadly snakes under his ledgers.

I decided to improvise a sequence with a spitting cobra. This very unusual and deadly snake does not inject his poison through a bite, but when he sees an enemy he spits his venom into its eye. The venom enters the capillaries of the eye and kills the prey very, very fast. The best defense against a spitting cobra is to wear glasses. Since tourists wear wrist watches, the spitting cobras are often confused and aim at the crystal of a watch, instead of at the eye.

We were trying to film a scene in which Harry Guardino would approach a cobra, not seeing it, and the cobra would rear up and spit. To accomplish this, my snake expert, wearing protective glasses, grabbed the cobra and threw him on the ground. We had a square glass mounted in front of the camera lens to photograph the spitting action. To our great surprise, the cobra did not rear up, and he refused to assume any threatening postures or to spit. As a matter of fact, he just lay down, making his body rigid, acting dead. My cobra expert told me that this was normal behavior. The snake was afraid of us, and thus he would keep that motionless position so he would not be bothered. Unfortunately, we had to bother him so that we could get our shot. Our snake man kicked him, first gently, then less gently, with the toe of his snake-bite-proof boots to get the snake moving. It took a good five minutes of kicking and shoving until the cobra got angry enough to bite into Harry Guardino's boots and spit at the camera. I learned a new lesson. Cobras are less mean than people.

Living in Africa, my sons and I lost our fear of snakes completely — which does not mean that we are not cautious. Still, we had a tough time making poisonous snakes and constrictors look aggressive for the film we made about them.

One night I was driving down a dirt road with Jan Oelofse and his Zulu assistant. In the light of our headlights we saw a sixteen-foot python slithering across the road. Oelofse stepped on the brake, jumped out of the car, then jumped on the snake, catching him by the neck. I followed and grabbed the tail of the big python. Our Zulu assistant was ready with a sack. Oelofse pushed the head of the snake into the sack. The snake took comfort in the darkness and disappeared into his newly found nest. We tied a rope around the sack and drove away with our catch. Now, whenever we needed shots of a big python, we would let him loose and photograph him swimming, climbing on trees, or attacking prey. Then, each time, we recaptured him. I learned from this that two fairly strong men can handle a giant snake up to twenty feet long. A snake has power only when it can anchor its tail onto a tree or something similar. Otherwise, one person is strong enough to hold its head while another holds its tail, thus rendering the snake nondangerous.

From Swaziland, we proceeded to Hartebeestport Dam where Jack Seale, one of the great snake experts of South Africa, lived. From here, we went together on a filming expedition to photograph the capture of the most poisonous snakes of the African continent. Our targets were the Egyptian cobra, Gaboon viper, puff adder, boomslang, and the black mamba. Among these, the mamba is the most feared. There are frightening stories about its bite. Every reptile book mentions that in the Boer War a black mamba reared up twelve feet high and bit a British cavalry soldier, who died instantly. In Natal, I heard that a truck drove over the tail of an eighteen-foot black mamba. The skinny brown-black snake reared up and hit nine sugarcane workers in the back of the truck. All died immediately.

Jack had ten black mambas in a snake pit. He told me and my cameramen that if we photographed them without moving our bodies there would be absolutely no danger, for a mamba will never strike a nonmoving target. My two cameramen stood for two hours among the slithering black devils. They are so agile that they can raise two-thirds of their length into the air. Most other snakes can rise only to one-third of their height. While we were filming, they looked right at us and kept slithering under our feet without showing any aggression. As a result we got some most interesting film sequences of snake life.

Soon after Jack assured us that mambas were not dangerous, he was bitten by a giant mamba while he was measuring its length. Jack threw the snake into a sack, knowing he had only three minutes to administer the antidote to himself. This is why there are usually no survivors of mamba bites. Jack succeeded in injecting himself with the necessary dosage. Then his skin began to tingle and he collapsed. An ambulance took him to the best hospital in Pretoria. Here he became conscious for a few seconds and instructed the doctor to put him in a heart and lung machine. Jack had once seen a guinea pig whose life was being prolonged in a heart and lung machine after it had been bitten by a mamba.

In a few minutes, Jack was placed in a heart and lung machine, and he then lived through the most eerie six days of his life. He was conscious but completely paralyzed. He saw everything and heard everything that his wife and the doctor were talking about. The doctor felt that Jack was clinically dead and that the heart and lung machine should be stopped. Jack's wife pleaded with him to continue. The doctor explained that there was severe brain damage from the poison, and that even if Jack survived he would be only a living vegetable. All of this Jack was experiencing as if he were outside his body, and there was nothing he could do. There was no way to give a sign that his mind was intact. On the seventh day, Jack's paralysis ended and he was fully recovered.

One reason I like to work with Jack is that he is completely fearless. He is so interested in snakes that he has continued to work with them, at the risk of losing his life.

One day on our snake expedition, we encountered a nine-foot Egyptian cobra. Fearing us, the cobra feigned death. Jack wanted to show me that the snake was actually paralyzed in this state. He picked the snake up like a long stick and kept throwing it up in the air. The cobra did not change its stiff posture. Then we decided to fool the snake, and we left it behind. Our Zulu assistant was instructed to climb a tree to watch the cobra and to signal us when it tried to sneak away.

When the cobra moved, we surrounded him, calling his bluff. This was too much for the cobra. His ruse discovered, he became furious and reared up and tried to hit us with his deadly fangs. Jack fought the snake the way a matador would fight a bull. Jack parried the snake's attacks and then extended a target with his left hand so that it was just a few inches from the snake's reach. When the cobra struck at Jack's left hand, he grabbed the snake's neck with his right hand and we had a captive cobra for our film.

The most famous snake expert in Africa was a Greek scientist named Ionides, who died a few years ago at the age of eighty-five. He supplied most of the zoos and pharmaceutical companies with poisonous snakes, and his home in the steaming jungle on the Tanganyikan coast was full of cobras and mambas in flimsy cages. The snakes got out regularly, but they never harmed Ionides, thus proving again that humans are not the targets of snakes.

While I was making the documentary on poisonous snakes, it was proved to me again and again that poisonous snakes are nonaggressive unless one steps on their tails or surprises them. Every snake we captured tried to get away from us rather than attack us. Of course, accidents happen, but the likelihood of an accident diminishes the more we understand of the natural history of the reptiles. We who live in nature often forget that lay people are not aware of some of the most obvious facts. For instance, all reptiles are deaf. They cannot hear us, so if we do not vibrate the ground with our feet, we do not alert them to our presence. For this reason, I shuffle my feet when walking through grass in the tropics.

In Africa, the young children who run around barefoot are the most frequent victims of snake bites. Whether a snake bite is deadly or not depends on whether the snake merely hits the victim with his needlelike fangs to scare him away, or if the snake is angry and thus chews after the bite. Chewing means that the snake presses the poison glands against the body of the victim and squirts a full load of poison into the wound. When this happens, the bite normally is fatal.

Some of the most poisonous snakes are very small, and they cannot open their mouths wide enough to bite into a good-sized limb. One such small snake is the boomslang. It has the deadliest of all poisons but can bite only into a toe or little finger, not into an arm or a leg.

My middle son, Peter, is the snake expert in the family. His bedroom in our house in Kenya was full of poisonous snakes as well as a nine-foot python. This python was a very ill-tempered creature who hated captivity and as soon as he was let out of his cage, he attacked Peter. Peter followed the Jack Seale method, presenting his left hand and wiggling his fingers as a target. As the python struck, Peter grabbed the neck of the python with his right hand. Every evening Peter performed for us on our porch. He was bitten only once. In this way, he acquired a skill that often proved very useful.

Later, we went on a filming expedition to the Chalbi Desert on the frontiers of Ethiopia. This is the home of the saw-scaled viper, a tiny snake that hides under palm leaves. There is no known antidote to its poison. While there, we lived in tents and our latrine was also in a tent. One day we heard a scream from the young actress who played the part of a scientist in the documentary I was filming. Peter ran into the small latrine tent, disregarding her privacy, and captured his first saw-scaled viper, which he kept in a jar and donated to the museum in Nairobi. Another time, we heard blood-curdling screams coming from the cook tent, and three cooks ran out. Peter entered

Peter Tors on the Orinoco with a pet

and tried to catch the mamba that had frightened our native help, but the mamba was too fast for him and so he had to kill it.

Snakes have a very interesting history in evolution. Between 120 million and 90 million years ago, a weather change killed most of the giant reptiles. Only those who could dig for a shelter could survive. Among those who survived, the biggest were the crocodiles and the great turtles. Some of the reptilians survived by living underground for millions of years, in the course of which their legs atrophied. Examining the skeleton of a snake, one can still find the tiny bones of vestigial legs and feet inherited from its lizard ancestry.

The snake is a very clean creature and the touch of a snake is sensual and pleasant. Unfortunately, the Bible gave them very bad publicity. Because they are not visible most of the time, people are afraid of them. What we don't know frightens us.

In 1973 I was invited to film some snake experiments at the Institute of Neurosciences at La Jolla, California. Many people do not realize it, but snakes smell with their forked tongues and have night vision through an infrared heat receptor organ. First, we demonstrated the existence of the heat sensory organ of the rattlesnake by tying five balloons to a rakelike device. One of the balloons was filled with warm water. Then the rattler was carefully blindfolded by experts, let loose in a terrarium, and threatened with the rake. The angry rattler immediately struck at the water-filled balloon instead of at the air-filled balloons. The reason was that the water-filled balloon was about the same temperature as any small mammal.

Holding the snake's head, Dr. Peter Hartline pointed out where the heat pits are located, between the snake's eyes and nostrils. The heat pits, two small holes, will admit two beams of heat emanating from any living creature or nearby object, and the two heat beams will meet on the lens-shaped wall of an inside cavity covered with infrared heat receptor cells. This membrane will act like an inside mirror, allowing the snake to "see" the heat image of the prey. It is an internal third eye for nighttime use — and most snakes are night hunters. This third eye gives them an advantage over the rodents they feed on. It is an incredible mechanism that nature has invented for the survival of the species.

Dr. Hartline next anesthetized a snake with Amytal Sodium. When it was in a deep sleep, Hartline and I blindfolded it. He then performed an intricate operation on the skull. Under a microscope, he bored a tiny hole and attached electrodes to certain specific nerve endings. Then he connected the wires to an oscilloscope and a loudspeaker. The amplifier produced a normal hum and the screen showed a normal steady wave.

Hartline now told me to pass my hand in front of the sleeping, blindfolded snake. As I made this movement about twelve inches away from the sleeping snake's heat organ, suddenly a busy, crazy pattern appeared on the screen. The low hum of the amplifier increased threefold till it became a cacophony — proof that, while the snake was sleeping, its unique mechanism was alert to the presence of living flesh in front of its head. This sensor gives the snake a tremendous advantage to strike out in the night and hit the prey.

The second experiment we witnessed had to do with snakes' sense of smell. All reptiles have flicking, forked tongues that function not as tasting but as smelling organs. With them, a snake picks up floating scent molecules. The molecules now attached to the tongue are carried back inside the mouth where the so-called Jacobsonian organ is located on the snake's upper palate. The tongue will sweep this organ, and the molecule of a single substance will fit into a matching opening, just as a key fits a lock. The nerve endings in the organ will then send the message to the brain, and the brain will decode the origin of the scent molecule. In this way, the snake can identify its prey in the night.

To demonstrate this, we went to a cage where laboratory mice were kept. We took a handful of litter from the bottom of the cage and took it to an empty terrarium with sawdust on the bottom. We sprinkled the litter into S-like patterns, then blindfolded a rattlesnake and dropped it on the sawdust. The blindfolded creature followed the S-like pattern as soon as it recognized the scent of the mouse. This Jacobsonian organ is so well developed in newborn snakes that they will strike at a swab of cotton scented with an extract of its future prey, such as a mouse or a rat.

Rats, mice, and other rodents would eat up our grain and rule the world without snakes to limit them. Thus, snakes protect us from worse things than snakes, such as famine. I hope you may now understand my liking of and fascination with snakes. They are much more complicated creatures than our common knowledge suggests.

11 Psychic Animals

THE PRECOGNITIVE ABILITIES of animals have intrigued me since early childhood, and a male Doberman pinscher named Lux was most responsible for my lifelong research. I met Lux in Budapest, where I went to school as a child. He belonged to my best friend, John. I loved Lux, who was the gentlest dog I ever met and who completely contradicted the fierce reputation of the Dobermans. He liked everything and everybody, except that he hated to take a bath. Every Friday night, John and I gave Lux a defleaing bath, and so every Friday night we had to go through the same circus. On that day, Lux would be missing. Because he could not get beyond the garden, after searching every nook and cranny, we would always find him under an old bedspread or somewhere in the garden among the dense bushes. It used to take us a good half hour to corner him and then to carry the unhappy Lux to the tub.

Thus, at the age of fourteen, I realized that Lux could tell Fridays from other days, because he hid from us on Fridays only. My pragmatic mind became intrigued, and I suggested to my friend that we should vary the days of Lux's defleaing baths. John agreed, and the following week we decided that Wednesday would be the day. When we returned from school that Wednesday, Lux was missing again. Searching through the garden, looking under every bed and behind every piece of furniture, we finally found him in the basement, hiding from us, trembling in fear of the defleaing bath. This was my first encounter with animal ESP or precognition.

Ten years later, now a young man living in California, I fell in love with a young lady who owned a Buick convertible and a wire-haired terrier. One Sunday afternoon, we were driving down Sunset Boulevard to the beach, and as we passed Doheny Drive, the terrier in the back suddenly went berserk. He kept jumping up and down, barking and whining as if warning us of something — which was most unusual behavior for this dog. A minute later, we had an explosive blowout in one of our tires, and if we had not, just before, slowed down because of the dog's crazy behavior, the open car could have turned over, injuring or killing us all.

Thirty years later, when my youngest son was twelve or thirteen, he owned an Australian sheep dog named Sheba. David and the dog had an extraordinarily close relationship. When David was at home, the dog always kept close to him. Once, when David was stricken by flu and had to stay in bed, the dog did not leave his bedside for twenty-four hours, restraining her bowels and bladder all that time.

My son came home from school every day at 3:30 P.M. Around 3:15, my wife could observe Sheba sneaking into the back yard, where she found an intricate way to get around and behind the garage, then to the front of the house, where she positioned herself awaiting David's arrival. This ritual was repeated every day.

One day when my wife was away, my son called me from school telling me that he had a dental appointment at 2:30 and asking whether I could drive him to the dentist if he came home at 2:00 instead of the usual 3:30. I told him that I would. That day I drove home from my office at 1:00 and asked the maid to make me a sandwich. I was reading *Scientific American* magazine and munching on my food and drinking a glass of milk when I noticed Sheba leaving my side and trying to get into the garden. The glass door was closed. She became agitated. I opened the door and observed Sheba going through her routine of sneaking around the back of the garage. At 1:55, Sheba took her usual place in front of the door and waited for David's arrival. She was aware that his normal arrival time had been changed.

In July 1967, George Gray, the superintendent of our animal farm, Africa USA, where we made the TV show *Daktari,* came into my Hollywood office. George was a burly, good-natured Australian who always came to the point. "Mr. Tors, we must build a new elephant house. The old one is too flimsy for the heavy winter we are expecting."

I was taken by surprise and said, "George, we are in California. The farm is ten miles from the Mojave Desert. Why would you expect a rough winter?"

George answered me laconically, "Come out and look at your zebras."

Two days later I visited the farm. We had a herd of twelve zebras. I examined each one. All of them carried a much heavier fur than normal for a zebra in the heat of July. As it turned out, the 1967–68 winter was a disaster. Eleven inches of rain fell in one day, the normal rainfall for a whole year. The dam above us burst and a ten-foot wave swept through our canyon, carrying away our studio, the *Daktari* sets, nine trucks, bulldozers, and other vehicles. It was a multimillion-dollar catastrophe. This all happened in March 1968, but the zebras had warned us in July 1967.

Luckily, we managed to save our animals in time — with the exception of my great bear, Gentle Ben. His enclosure was washed away by the flood, and we later found the broken cage ten miles downstream. We were positive that Gentle Ben was dead. We were wrong. Seven days later, he ambled back good naturedly, guided by his homing instinct, through the broken gate, looking for his cage and friends.

In 1965, I directed an MGM picture for young people, titled *Zebra in the Kitchen.* I needed a house cat for the first scene,

Ivan Tors and his animals at Africa USA (*Bill Ray, Life Magazine,* © 1967 *Time, Inc.*)

so I picked up a calico cat at Africa USA and took her in my station wagon to Culver City. Our first shot was of a cat perched on a chimney as an escaped tiger approaches. The cat takes a good look at the tiger and runs. As we photographed the scene, the cat not only ran upon seeing the tiger, but leaped from the roof to the ground, climbed a ten-foot fence to Washington Boulevard, and disappeared into the morning traffic.

Africa USA was sixty miles from Culver City, separated from Los Angeles by a range of 7000-foot-high mountains and the Bakersfield Freeway, a ten-lane highway with traffic of 50,000 cars a day. The cat had very little chance of finding home without getting killed. Nevertheless, six weeks later, the calico cat arrived back at Africa USA.

Interested in the sense of locality that animals have, I conducted certain experiments under the supervision of a distinguished zoologist from UCLA, Professor Fred White, now with the Scripps Institution of Oceanography. For one of our many experiments, we took a young red deer in a truck from a farm to a mountain where he had never been before, and let him go.

We were picked up by a helicopter so we would not leave tracks behind us. The mountain was forested, and there was no way for the deer to observe the farm by sight or smell. Three hours later the deer was back at the farm.

Fascinated by animal ESP, I began collecting anecdotal material, such as reports that six hours before the great earthquake in Sarajevo, Yugoslavia, the animals in the zoo there became restless and agitated and made attempts to get out of their enclosures.

A woman in Tashkent reported that her dog dragged her out of her house just before the ground began to shake. Ants hoisted their eggs on their backs and began a mass migration. Mountain goats and antelopes in the zoo refused to enter indoor pens, and tigers began to sleep in the open before a big earthquake in Siberia, although scientific instruments had not yet registered any disturbance.

In Kamchatka, in the USSR, where a volcano violently erupted in the winter of 1955, not a single bear was killed. All had come out of hibernation in their respective caves and moved into safer areas days before any volcanic activity was noted on the seismograph.

The migration, the movement of animals, has always been motivated by instinct to escape unfavorable climatic and feeding conditions or other threats to their lives. Probably, migration behavior originated during the ice ages, when birds had to move south because they could not feed on the insects through the ice pack that covered the earth. So, in their primitive brains, they developed receptors that analyze signals from the cosmos indicating threatening changes. It is possible that humans may have possessed the same kind of receptors, but civilization has made us forget how to use such decoding mechanisms. On the other hand, supersensitive humans still may be able to do so.

In my research work and travels around the world, I have witnessed many so-called navigation miracles. I visited Dr. Archie Carr in Costa Rica, in the Bay of Turtles. Dr. Carr, a research professor from the University of Florida, has his research station on a long stretch of beach where thousands of giant green turtles appear in the summer months to lay their eggs, driven by instinct or by some biological guidance system. The first night of my arrival, we walked down on the beach with a flashlight. We observed a giant female green turtle emerging from the ocean waves after a thousand-mile, or longer, swim. She made her way up a sand dune and dug a one-foot-deep hole with her strong flipperlike hind legs. When the hole was deep enough, she began to lay her eggs, which were the size of Ping-Pong balls. In a few hours, the green turtle had laid about fifty eggs, which she covered with sand. Her job done, she was ready to return to the sea. At this point, scientific research interfered. It took three of us to turn the heavy turtle on her back. Thus immobilized, we could observe that she was already tagged. From the tag number we established that the same female had laid her eggs in the near vicinity of this location twice before in the past six years. The beach here is eighty miles long; how could this turtle find the very same spot in the dark of the night after two long years, coming from a distance of at least one thousand miles? After tagging her again, we turned her right side up and let her go back into the sea.

Our research with the monarch butterfly was even more impressive. We did our studies in the small community of Pacific Grove, California, just south of Monterey. Pacific Grove is considered the butterfly capital of the world. Each fall, hordes of monarch butterflies arrive from Canada, about twelve-hundred miles away, and mass in great festoons on the cypress trees, where they mate. As spring approaches, the butterflies begin a return journey to Canada, laying their eggs and breeding in places where milkweed is found. From tagging studies, we found that subsequent generations return to the same tree and that the butterfly travels from fifty to eighty miles a day. These fragile butterflies can complete a two-thousand-mile journey in about a month's time. How do they know the direction, how do they find the same grove and the same trees, how come they are not swept away by strong winds? This direction-finding miracle cannot be explained by scientific means, at least not yet. Another "sense" is indicated — a sense of locality connected with precognition.

Here is yet another striking example of this seemingly psychic sense that animals have. My friend Harold Sherman lives with his wife in a log cabin in Mountain View, Arkansas, in the heart of the beautiful Ozarks. One day, a dog appeared at the cabin and took up residence under the porch. When the dog refused to leave, the Shermans checked the expensive collar that bore his name and address. The dog belonged to the Burns family in Eugene, Oregon. Oregon being very far from Arkansas, Harold assumed that the Burns family was visiting in the Ozarks and that their dog had wandered away. After a few phone calls to the neighboring farms, he located the Burnses. They were visiting from Oregon, and they were looking for their dog. Harold gave them directions, and within an hour the Burnses arrived to pick up their errant pooch. Upon their arrival, they were absolutely dumbfounded. The Sherman's cabin had belonged to them forty years ago. From there, they had moved to Oregon after the dog's great-grandfather had been born on this farm. Although the descendant dog had never been in the Ozarks and so had never seen the cabin before, he had sought it out through some instinct and had established himself where his ancestors were born. We are most unsure of how to explain what attracted the dog to the cabin, but there are two distinct possibilities.

One is that scent molecules of the owners were still present nearly forty years later, having been "inscribed" in the locality. Dogs have an extremely refined olfactory organ and can read scent molecules as if they were sign posts. The other possibility, far-fetched as it may sound, is that there is a genetic memory of locality and gravitational forces. Just like déjà vu in parapsychology.

Geneticists have proved this with fruit flies. They have fed different groups of fruit flies with sugar water in plastic tubes that have been positioned at different angles. That is, the first tube was placed horizontally, the second was raised to a ten-degree angle, the third had a twenty-degree elevation, etc. Scientists found that the offspring of the original fruit flies, even after four or five generations, preferred feeding tubes that were elevated at the same angle as their ancestors' tubes had been. This genetic memory may not be conscious, but in the unconscious the creature feels safe and secure in such specific, "familiar" localities.

Another miracle of nature is the ability of certain spiders to spin their webs two hours before sunrise so the unfinished web will not dry out in the rays of the sun. During daylight hours these spiders do only repair work. The time of the rising sun varies from day to day, just like the tides. So how does a spider know when it is two hours before sunrise?

Of course, all these heretofore inexplicable animal mysteries may have a scientific explanation once we understand our true nature. For instance, if we look into the sun, we perceive only a single beam of light, but when we look into the sun through a prism, we see red, orange, yellow, green, blue, indigo, and violet light beams. Likewise, when we dissect any mammal, we find under the skin a lymph system, skeleton, heart, lung, liver, spleen, esophagus, tongue, urinary tract connected to the kidney, and so on. Most of these parts of the body are functioning continuously without the mammal being aware of them. It is easily possible that all creatures possess a mechanism, possibly even on the cellular level, that is connected to the cosmos — past, present, and future — and receives signals to warn us when survival is affected, because all living things are survival-oriented. Somewhere in our limbic system we may carry such a biological, silent alarm.

But, as we know, not all such mysteries remain unsolved forever. For instance, we were puzzled for a long time by the rat's ability to avoid radiation. Later we learned that radiation creates ozone, and ozone has a smell similar to the smell that is in the air after lightning strikes. This smell tips off the rat. Of course, the nose of a human is not as sensitive as a rat's. Although we cannot smell a few molecules of ozone, the rat can, and so it avoids danger.

My annual visits to the game farm in Namibia (South-West Africa) have revealed other interesting animal mysteries. Around my son Steve's house there were three ostriches whose mother was killed by a cheetah when they were tiny. Steve had brought them home to protect them from predators, and they had grown to full size. In 1976, I was making a film around the game farm, and the behavior of these ostriches completely puzzled me. They never returned to the bush to join other ostriches, but always stayed near the house. The land is full of hills and thorn trees, so these giant birds cannot see too far. Their sense of smell is negligible compared to that of mammals. Still, no matter where we happened to be filming beyond the fences surrounding the 75,000 acres, which was completely outside their range of smell or vision, the ostriches would appear in an incredibly short time, indicating that they had not followed our tire marks on the road but had come to us in a straight line. It never failed. The ostriches always knew immediately where we were. Fences or other obstacles did not stop them. Please don't ask me how they did it, for I haven't the faintest idea — but that's what I call a sense of locality!

In 1972, I made a film for NBC on the plight of the elephants in an area where there had been no rainfall for thirteen months. If they were to survive, the elephants would have either to find the last existing water holes or to dig their own in dried out riverbeds. I followed the herds in a helicopter at high altitudes. One day I spotted a herd in rough, hilly country, heading for a water hole about thirty miles away on the Mozambique border.

The water hole was not within range of vision or scent, and there was no direct path to it through the rocky hills. Still, the elephants marched in a straight line, moving on without hesitation, knowing exactly where they were heading. They kept pushing through obstacles rather than going around them, as though being guided by a radio compass.

I had similar experiences with homing pigeons in Switzerland, where I met Professor Gerhard Wagner, the foremost authority on homing pigeons, who had about a hundred fifty Belgian blues under observation at the time. He placed six pigeons in a basket and covered them up so that no visual orientation was possible. Then he took them aboard the Swiss army helicopter he used for his experiments. The chopper zigzagged among the peaks of the Jura Mountains as he flew to a point about a hundred fifty miles away. Here he released the birds from the helicopter while still in flight. Then we followed them and observed them at a distance of a few hundred yards. What did we learn? First, the pigeons flew high up, surveying the terrain. Then they landed near a farm that had structures similar to those at Dr. Wagner's home. After landing, they realized their mistake and so they flew high again until they noted the valley near Bern, where Dr. Wagner lived. It was almost evening by that time, and so they did not take off again, but stayed at the edge of a forest until the next morning. In the morning, the sky was heavily overcast and the visibility was limited. The pigeons took off again and, as if realizing that visual orientation was impossible, they shifted into another navigational system we do not understand. Now they flew around the Jura Mountains without any difficulty and reached their loft at Dr. Wagner's home before evening. Their flight had shifted from visual to instrument flying, as a pilot would put it. What are the instruments and where might they be located in our survival system? We are still too ignorant to understand, although the finest brains in physiology have been working to find the answers for many, many years.

Migratory restlessness had already been observed long ago by Darwin. Birds with their wings pinioned or with injured legs will try to hop in the right compass direction when the time for migration arrives. The swallows of Capistrano well know their time for taking off and their time to return. They never miss the day. But not all of them make it home, which proves that navigational ability and sensitivity to force fields, or other signals from the cosmos, will differ between individual birds just as levels of intelligence differ between people.

On June 1, 1977, I returned to Los Angeles from South America, where I had directed a film in the Orinoco jungle. Since I had not heard for many months from my son Steven, the first thing I wanted to do was to telephone him. I was about to dial the overseas operator, when suddenly I suffered a muscle cramp in my right leg that caused me unbearable pain. I screamed and could do nothing but massage the contracting knot in my muscle until the spasm stopped and I was relieved from the excruciating pain. I have suffered from very few cramps in my life so this was a most unusual experience. Finally, I was in a condition to dial, to reach the operator and ask her to get me the telephone number in Namibia. Through the communications satellite, I was connected with my son's residence immediately.

My son's best friend answered the phone. "Steven is not here," I heard him say. "Steve was shot. But don't worry, he'll be all right." Then he related the story of the accident. My son had been catching giant antelopes by driving them into a net. As he tried to untangle the horns of a bull eland, the animal pushed against him and Steven's revolver popped out of his holster and discharged. A soft-nosed bullet entered his calf from above and came out just over his ankle. It was exactly the same place where I had my cramp before calling him.

"It was his left leg, wasn't it?" I asked deliberately.

The answer was, "No, it was his right leg." And that's where my pain had struck.

I know now that the supernatural is a part of nature, as are migration, dolphin sonar, and the infrared vision of snakes. Half of my son's genes are my own, and these are probably in harmony with my wavelength, my force fields. So when his survival is threatened, an alarm signal goes off in me.

African game guards have often told me that they do not need a radio. In the primitive world of the African bush, desert, and jungle, they know where they are needed.

My conclusion, after a lifetime of research and study and after having been a skeptic for some twenty to thirty years, is that we exist on a single conscious level and on multiple subconscious levels. Our conscious level is only the tip of the iceberg. Four-fifths of our life forces are not visible to us or to others, but they constitute our essence, our race, our memories, our cosmic connections, our belief systems, our feelings, and premonitions. Our survival system is anchored not only in the past, but in the future. Precognition is not easy to understand with our neocortex. Our recently developed brain, which is opportunistic, helps us to function day to day but cannot envision too deeply or too far without the all-important assistance of a universal wisdom that exists in all of us without being apparent to many of us.

It may sound naive, but I hold to be true that we are interconnected with each other, with each living thing, with everything that exists in the cosmos yesterday, today, and tomorrow, and that love is one of the forces that connects all of us. Love exists just as gravity or magnetism does. Love can pass through time and space. Love changes the flow of adrenalin. Adrenalin changes the electrical conductivity of the human system and modulates our electric fields. Sympathetic force fields of other bodies may very well receive these pulses. In my opinion, telepathy, precognition, and paranormal sensitivity are essential parts of our survival systems. To quote Dr. Barbara Brown, the mother of biofeedback, "The highest order of intellectual capacities — elegant and sophisticated — reside in what we call the unconscious and may always reside there because they are unrecognized by society."

12   Learning from Dolphins

IN THE FOREWORD of this book, I mentioned that I lost my human arrogance after working with animals. I believe that every living being has its own view of reality, and that view can be very different from the reality seen by another creature. A fly with compound eyes and feet that can hear conceives of the world very differently from a human or any other animal. A worm inside an apple thinks that his world is the apple. When it eats itself through to the skin and finds itself in a bag of apples, it will believe that the world is the bag, and so on. Humans are no different. Every day our world enlarges. The cosmos gets bigger. Science expands our knowledge and perception, and this learning process makes life interesting for the curious.

Among all animal life, dolphins have contributed most to my better understanding of other kinds of intelligence. I have learned that men are not superior, only different. I have learned that an animal can possess a logic apart from Pavlovian conditioning and can have compassion and a cooperative spirit, not only toward his own species, but toward other species as well — and that includes us.

Two unusual people introduced me to the world of dolphins — Ricou Browning and Dr. John Lilly. While photographing *Sea Hunt* in Silver Springs, Florida, I needed extra divers, and Bill Ray of Silver Springs Resort recommended that I employ Ricou, his publicity chief, a silent, good-looking athlete.

Watching the operation of my group, I soon noticed that the most dependable and competent diver of all my people was Ricou, who impressed me so much that, after two days, I put him in charge of all diving operations. He subsequently worked with me as underwater director and chief of diving operations through more than a hundred episodes of *Sea Hunt,* two *Flipper* features, eighty-eight TV episodes of *Flipper,* and all my other underwater films.

Ricou was a serious young man, and I always took him seriously. However, I must confess that in the beginning I had some doubts about his sanity. He told me incredible stories about his personal experiences with dolphins, beginning with the capture of a freshwater dolphin in the Amazon, where he had gone on an expedition to catch snakes for the Silver Springs reptile exhibit. When the dolphin, which he kept in a small lagoon next to his house, died a year later, Ricou took the loss as a great personal tragedy. I thought at the time that he had overdramatized the whole incident, but later, as I got to know Ricou Browning better, I realized that he never overdramatized anything.

After our success with *Sea Hunt,* Ricou wanted me to make a film on dolphins. He and Jack Cowden, a radio writer, wrote a film treatment titled *Flipper* and submitted it to me for consideration. I was intrigued by the story, and I wanted to learn more about dolphins, so I arranged a meeting with the top dolphin expert, Dr. John Lilly, head of the Communications Research Institute in Miami.

At this time, there was very little general knowledge about dolphins. In some aquariums, they were trained like dogs by former lion trainers who were unaware of the superior intelligence of dolphins. Dr. Lilly's scientific accomplishments in many fields are legendary. He is a graduate of the California

Institute of Technology, has a medical degree from the University of Pennsylvania, and was the foremost brain researcher of the National Institute of Mental Health. His outstanding research with monkey brains established him as a top neurophysiologist, and he also became known for his pioneering research in sensory deprivation. But he gave up almost everything else for the study of dolphins once he got acquainted with this fabulous species.

What I learned from dolphins, and what Dr. Lilly taught me, was that we are not alone at the top of the evolutionary scale; that there are other large-brained creatures, such as whales, dolphins, and elephants, with brains comparable to the human brain. And I learned that, for the last fifteen million years, these creatures have used logic and cooperation and have lived by ethical standards. For instance, once I was at the Marineland of the Pacific when a diver was inside a five-hundred-thousand-gallon tank, cleaning the windows. The tank contained some moray eels and a few dolphins. For no good reason, an aggressive moray eel bit into the leg of the diver. A second later, a dolphin dove down, picked up the six-foot eel

Flipper in the Bahamas (*Metro-Goldwyn-Mayer*)

with his jaws, then came to the surface and threw the offending eel out of the tank, in hopes that the eel would now learn not to offend anyone. This gesture meant that the dolphin had passed judgement, had protected the man that fed him, and still had acted within the limits of civilized behavior, without killing the eel.

Dolphin logic was made evident to me when I was playing with Flipper, throwing balls from the dock to her in her lagoon, training her to retrieve them. (Yes, Flipper was in reality a "she.") As a behaviorist, I immediately observed that this dolphin was an experimenter — unlike a dog, which would always retrieve a ball in the same way. The first time, she did retrieve it like a dog, between her teeth; but the next time, she tucked the ball under a flipper; the third time, she pushed it with her bottle-shaped nose; and the fourth time, she created a water flow with one of her flippers, and the water pressure pushed the ball to the dock. Then, what I consider a miracle happened. I had two balls in my hand, a small one and a much bigger one. I threw the big one to her, and she was waiting for it with gaping jaws. Accidentally, my aim was too good, so the bigger ball landed right in her mouth. I threw the small ball immediately afterward. As I threw it, Flipper released the bigger ball, realizing that, because of the shape of her jaws, she could not hold both balls at the same time if the big one was already in place. So she then picked up the small one first, and next the big one again. This way, her jaws could hold both balls at once. She brought them back to me in one sweep. Her feat of logic, an instant decision that her jaws could hold the balls only if the small one was on the bottom, proved to me that this creature was not an ordinary animal. A human child could not have figured it out, and some adults probably would have taken a longer time than Flipper took. From then on I spent many hours studying dolphin behavior — either with Flipper at our lagoon or else in Dr. Lilly's institute.

I soon learned that we humans, as primates, learn slowly by play instinct. The dolphins are way ahead of us; they are instant learners. Teaching a dolphin a trick is easy if we can work out how to communicate what we want. For instance, we once needed a scene in which Flipper was to tow a dinghy full of children by the tow line. I was dead sure that it would take a long time to train a dolphin to do that, but how wrong I was! Ricou took a length of nylon rope, made a noose at one end and threw it to Flipper. Flipper pushed her nose through the noose and brought it back to the dock. Then Ricou filled the dinghy with children and told Steve, my eldest son, who was then six years old, to throw the line into the water at his command. Ricou pushed the dinghy away from the dock, and when it floated about thirty feet out, Ricou gave his command. Steve dropped the noose end of the line into the water. Flipper's sonar picked up the splash and in the next two seconds she reached the side of the dinghy, pushed her nose through the noose, and towed the boat back to the dock where Ricou and I were standing. She was rewarded by a fish, and from then on, as long as we produced *Flipper,* the dolphin towed the boat wherever we wanted it, as soon as the noose was dropped into the ocean.

Another time, I bought thirty butterfish, Flipper's favorite, for the next day's shooting. The fish were in a purse-shaped net, the bottom of which was pulled tight by a line with a lead weight attached to it, in order to keep Flipper away from the fish until the next day. I hung the purse in the lagoon so that the fish would stay alive, and Flipper watched the procedure. She then lined up with the purse and sounded it. "Sounding" means emitting short clicks of the dolphin sonar. The sounding gave her all the answers she needed. Pulling on the lead weight would have only tightened the line, so she took the weight between her teeth and pushed against it, thus loosening the line and letting a butterfish swim free. Flipper immediately pulled the purse string tight and then caught the butterfish. Had she left the net open, all the butterfish could have escaped, and she might have gotten only two or three of the lot. After she caught the single escapee and ate it, she returned and continued the procedure. Open purse; let one fish out; close purse tightly; eat fish; and so on. Her logic was incredible. Later we observed other behavior patterns that were even more astounding.

One day, Mr. Santini, a Florida Keys fisherman, captured five dolphins for our film, and we placed them in a fenced-off enclosure in the ocean. We decided to train several dolphins in addition to Flipper. We separated one of the dolphins, a six-foot female, from the others, and I went into the water in an attempt to establish a relationship while Dr. Lilly looked on.

The dolphin had just had a bad experience with the cruel humans who had captured her, and so she avoided contact. (Had she wished to, the dolphin could have killed me with one blow of her powerful nose, but dolphins are usually nonviolent, except when defending their newborn offspring against sharks.) Then suddenly she became entangled in the net that separated her from the other side of the enclosure. Dolphins are air-breathing mammals, and if they cannot rise to the surface, they will drown just like a human. Dr. Lilly realized the

Steven Tors (fist in his mouth) and Peter Tors (straw hat) watch Luke Halpin communicate with Flipper (*Metro-Goldwyn-Mayer*)

danger and shouted to me, "Raise her head out of the water." I did what he said, lifting the entangled dolphin in my arms above the water level so that she could breathe. Dr. Lilly gave me other commands: "Disentangle her slowly. While you do it, stroke her very softly. She must learn that your skin is smooth and not sandpapery like shark skin." I did what John said. The skin of dolphins is very sensitive and vulnerable. Their great sonar equipment helps them avoid coral, the bottom, in fact anything that can scratch. All dolphins are hemophiliacs, or bleeders — that is, their blood does not clot easily. Thus their sonar must alert them to rough surfaces.

I took a good ten minutes to disengage the dolphin, with a kind of loving gentleness. When the dolphin was free, she was not afraid of me any longer. At that, my middle son, Peter (at the time, only five years old), saw his father playing with a big dolphin, and he jumped into the water with me. Then came a miracle of the century, later described in a number of scientific books. Pete's size was about the size of a baby dolphin. The big female dove and came up with Peter on her back. Pete held on to her dorsal fin and rode the dolphin, crisscrossing the lagoon. The ancient myth became a reality in front of our eyes. We were all choked up with emotion. A boy riding a dolphin. My little boy! The maternal instinct of the female dolphin had crossed the boundary between two different species.

From then on, it became routine to photograph Flipper towing Luke Halpin, our boy actor, or Luke riding on Flipper's back. Now that we knew that it could be done, this behavior became a regular stunt in our series, and it may have been the key to our success with *Flipper*. The recognition that a warm relationship can develop between children and dolphins made it beautiful.

In my long association with dolphins, I had an opportunity to observe their courting habits, their lovemaking, the birth of their babies, and their intercommunication. I witnessed a young male courting a young female in the ocean in a perfect ballet scene. They were swimming figure eights on the ocean surface, gently touching each other with their flippers, sometimes in the genital area. We heard a series of sounds emitting from the blowholes, probably expressions of "I love you." This kind of foreplay may last for days and days. When they are properly aroused, they will rub against each other until an erect and slightly curved organ appears from the male's genital slit — not very different from a human organ. As they swim together, belly to belly, the male will thrust his organ into the female's cavity, and the marriage will be consummated.

The gestation period is between eleven and twelve months. Toward the end of her term, the mother selects her best friend to be her nanny. She then spends less time with the school and more time alone with her girl friend. All dolphins are born tail first. Since dolphins are air-breathing mammals, the baby dolphin would drown if the head came out first. When the birth takes place, all dolphins are very excited and crowd around the mother because help is often needed. The umbilical cord has to be snapped and the baby has to be pushed to the surface for the first breath of air. This shoving must be repeated, because the dolphin's breathing is not a reflex reaction but rather a cognitive function. Underwater the blowhole is closed, and when the dolphin is out of air, it surfaces. The skin around the blowhole dries instantly and this dryness makes the blowhole open for another breath. The dolphin has to think about surfacing and breathing.

After the birth, the whole school stays together to protect the baby from sharks. While dolphins cannot smell, sharks can. Nothing tastes sweeter to a shark than a newborn dolphin. But if and when a shark approaches, the largest of the dolphins springs into action. Dolphins can swim at a speed of up to twenty miles an hour, and with their sledgehammerlike noses they can hit a shark with debilitating force in the area where the liver and spleen are located. Such an attack will, at the least, injure a shark enough so that it will no longer be a threat to the family of dolphins.

Three dolphins do a back tail-walk for Zale Parry during the filming of Ivan Tors's *Danny and the Mermaid* (*Miami Seaquarium*)

It was often observed that when a newborn dies, the mother will remain on the surface, with the baby in her jaws, hoping that the fresh air will revive her newborn. Sometimes, when the birth is difficult and the inner lining of the vagina does not slip back in place, other dolphins will, with their long noses, try to push the protrusion back where it belongs. At Marineland of California, once when such a difficult birth took place, not only did the dolphins help, but a false killer whale tried to assist the mother as well. Another time, when an adult dolphin died, a big male pilot whale picked up the dolphin in his jaws and carried her for days and days. It was most difficult to separate the whale from his small dead friend.

I have come to believe that the dolphins' world is better than our own, and that once we learn to communicate with them, there will be a lot we can learn from our large-brained underwater relatives. Dolphin-to-man communication was the goal of the Communication Research Institute (in Miami and the Virgin Islands), of which Dr. Lilly was in charge. Knowing my fascination with dolphins, he tried to share his scientific knowledge with me and invited me to join his institute so I could learn more about dolphin communication. I donated a dolphin to his laboratory, and he named it Peter, after my son. Peter became the first dolphin to try to imitate human sounds. He had learned how to call his attractive trainer, Margaret, whenever he was hungry. This was the first recorded attempt at vocal communication between different species, and the sound tape was played at many scientific conventions. It demonstrated the dolphins' eagerness to speak to us, even though their vocal frequency is entirely different from our own, which necessitates an enormous effort on their part to utter human sounds.

To do his research, Dr. Lilly did an experiment that involved putting a male and a female in separate tanks and placing a hydrophone in each tank. In this way, he hoped to pick up conversations between "husbands" and "wives." He succeeded. We are able to observe the resultant ultra high frequency communication on oscilloscopes — but we could not decode it. Apparently, the dolphins were able to conduct a conversation at two frequency levels at the same time. The patterns were photographed, then analyzed by experts, but we apelike land animals were not smart enough to understand what the dolphins were saying. I was sure that they were not complimenting us, for, whenever we passed their tanks, they squirted us with water — probably as punishment for our unauthorized, unethical eavesdropping. After all, dolphins, too, have a right to some privacy.

The end of the Communication Institute came when the good doctor began to feel guilty for keeping these intelligent creatures as captives. One day, he let his dolphins go free, and the institute closed down. I understood him. Those of us who worked with dolphins will never be the same.

My first awareness of a dolphin's dependence on sonar was in the Bahamas, where we built holding pens for our dolphins.

At Lyford Key we had about a three-acre area fenced off in twenty feet of water. With a net, we split the holding pen into two sections to separate a male from a female. Suddenly the female dolphin died. We lifted her out of the sea and removed the dividing net to give our male more living space. To my great surprise, the male dolphin remained in his part of the holding pen and did not cross the line where the net used to be. This behavior indicated to me that the male dolphin had made a map of the area with his sonar, and the map was firmly etched in his mind. It took the male dolphin a week's time before he crossed the imaginary line. In the meantime, his visual and sonic perception had had to be readjusted. Although dolphins have good eyesight, they depend on sonar first and sight second. Sonar works in darkness, and thus, muddy or turbulent waters will not distract them. Their sonar, or echolocation, acts as radar. The mechanism of the sonar is built into their skeletal structure in the form of two vibrating chambers in the skull — one at the end of the bottle-shaped nose and the other on top of the head, next to the blowhole. These two chambers will emit sound pulses in a conical direction, meaning that, as the dolphin swims, a cone of sound pulses precedes him, and the returning sound pulses tell exactly what faces him ahead — fish, coral, a ship, a shark — and how far it is. The modulated pulse penetrates matter, and the returning pulse tells not only the size of the discovered object but the texture as well. Thus, dolphin sonar can tell one kind of fish from another, even if the size or shape is the same.

The cone of sound pulses that originates from the blowhole scans the water above the dolphin, telling the dolphin what moves overhead and how far up the surface of the ocean is. Although the dolphin's brain is even larger than the human brain, and more convoluted, the auditory nerve endings occupy the largest part, completely overlapping the olfactory area — and this is the reason why dolphins and whales cannot smell. They've given up one sense to perfect another.

In 1973 I made experiments with dolphins to check their

sonar. In Queensland, Australia, I worked with a dolphin named Smiley. We placed rubber suction cups on Smiley's eyes so she was totally blinded. Having no sight or sense of smell, she had to retrieve objects by echolocation. I used round frames and square frames made out of the same plastic. Smiley was rewarded only when she retrieved a round object. Whenever a frame was thrown into the water, Smiley buzzed it. If it was square, she let it float. When she found it to be round, she retrieved it immediately. Although totally blinded, she knew where I was standing. She never made a single mistake.

After this set of experiments, I tried to deceive the blindfolded Smiley by taking her favorite fish and duplicating it out of different materials, such as wood, plastic, metal, plaster of Paris. Whenever we threw a fish into the water, Smiley would swim to it, buzz it, and take it into her mouth only if it was the genuine fish. She never touched a make-believe fish that was created for her deception.

We can understand some of the secret of Smiley's sonar, but not all of it. While she was underwater and blindfolded, she sometimes obeyed hand signals I gave her as I stood on the dock. So there may be even more to this perception than sonar alone. A good friend of mine, a marine biologist who trained dolphins while going through school, related to me an experience that would also indicate that dolphins perhaps have some form of extrasensory perception. Whenever he approached the holding tank of his dolphins, they would rise out of the water to wait for him — even if he was a half mile away and still out of their view. They would be impatiently standing on their tails, waiting, having somehow sensed his approach. We still know too little about dolphins and too little about ourselves to know how and why.

One of my incredible experiences with a dolphin occurred in September of 1963 in the Bahamas, when the first *Flipper* film had already been made. I had been away from the United States for a long period of time while making a film in Africa.

When I returned to the Bahamas, my crew was breaking in a new female dolphin named Suzy.

The training took place in a good-sized, deep lagoon, which had its exit to the ocean blocked by a giant net. It was stormy my first day, and the waves ran six or seven feet high. Of course, there are no waves underwater, and the bad weather bothered neither the dolphin nor the divers in their underwater work. I was anxious to meet the new "Flipper," so I put on my scuba gear and jumped into the water to get acquainted with Suzy.

Suzy completely snubbed me, swimming quickly past me and not allowing me to touch her. I wanted to stroke her — the first step in establishing a relationship with a dolphin — but she eluded me whenever I got close to her. Since I had not dived for a year, I was out of practice and soon became exhausted by the futile chase.

My regulator did not supply me with enough compressed air, so I had to surface to rest and breathe. As I surfaced and removed my mouthpiece to take a deep breath, a seven-foot wave hit me, and I swallowed at least a half gallon of salt water, which only made me more exhausted, nauseated, and hungry for air. Emitting the salt water made me sick to my stomach. As I tried to breathe again, another big wave hit me. The weather really became foul now. I swallowed more salt water and started to feel dizzy and weak. I was on the verge of passing out. I tried to scream for help when suddenly I felt Suzy's body between my legs. Instinctively I held onto her dorsal fin for support. This was the first time she had allowed me to touch her. Now she began to swim with me toward the shore, towing me to our diving ladder, and placing her head between two rungs of the ladder, making it easy for me to climb up on a rock where our diving equipment was stored.

Reaching safe shore, my first inclination was to praise God, who created this incredible, big-brained mammal that has charity toward man and the ability to know when she is needed.

My training crew was witness to Suzy's act. From the day of my rescue, Suzy and I were the best of friends, and she later became the star of the *Flipper* TV series.

Nearly twenty-four hundred years ago, Aristotle recognized the astounding intelligence and compassion of dolphins and described these characteristics in his *De Natura;* but until recently very little further inquiry took place. Of the many books and monographs that have now been written about dolphins, the best, in my opinion, is the work of a New Zealand historian named Antony Alpers. His book *The Dolphin — the Myth and the Mammal* relates some of the fabulous legends about the dolphins. Many Greek and Roman writers, among them Pliny the Elder, considered them to be man's best friend and described how they had carried children to school over waterways, rescued poets from pirates, saved sailors from drowning, and helped fishermen catch fish. Once, while walking in the catacombs under Rome, I noticed the shape of a dolphin on

Zale Parry swims with the bottle-nosed dolphin Pedro during the filming of *Danny and the Mermaid (Miami Seaquarium)*

the wall of a chamber where the early Christians once gathered. I asked the monk who was my guide what the sign of the dolphin meant to the Christians. His answer was, "Charity to Man."

The legend of the dolphin's charity to man was revived again in this century. Besides my own experience with Suzy, two similar cases were reported in Florida — again, exhausted swimmers were pushed to the shore by gentle dolphins. I talked to a water skier who swore to me that, when he fell off his skis, he was surrounded by sharks, but a school of dolphins came to his rescue, chasing the sharks away. Two Japanese sailors reported that when their boat sank on the high seas, dolphins assisted them in reaching land. A Navy life raft was allegedly pushed to the beach by dolphins after a shipwreck. We often hear such reports of dolphin miracles.

In regard to the legends, I asked the opinion of the top authority, and Dr. Lilly speculated that in the time of Aristotle and Pliny, the climate was much milder in the Mediterranean area than it is today. Therefore, more people were swimming then and more time was spent on the seashores, which resulted in many encounters with the dolphins. In this century, in the age of boating and water sports and the population explosion, man has renewed his acquaintance with the dolphins and has a new opportunity to observe these magnificent creatures and make friends with them.

I have discussed with Dr. Lilly the reason why the dolphin is a gentler creature than other mammals. He believes that the dolphin is a near-perfect being. It is faster than most fish and, with its sonar, has an easy time locating food. Because it does not have to compete with others, the dolphin has no reason to be aggressive except in defense of its young or each other.

Once, however, we had to put this tendency to a special test. I had been asked by MGM to produce a second Flipper feature under the title *Flipper and the Pirates*. When the screenplay was finished, I flew to the Bahamas to have a conference with

Ricou Browning, who was in charge of training Suzy to be Flipper. I told him that, in the film, Flipper would have to attack a pirate. Ricou felt that this would not be an easy task, because Suzy is a lover by nature and not an aggressor. "But dolphins are so smart," he added, "I'm sure we can teach her to act aggressively, it just may take a long time."

Next morning we were all at the training lagoon. Ricou wore the striped shirt of a pirate and had a rubber knife in his hand. As Ricou entered the crystal clear water, we witnessed another manifestation of Suzy's sensitivity to our needs. Suzy, who was Ricou's pet dolphin and usually greeted him affectionately, seemed to be in a different mood this time. She made fast and dangerous passes at him, scaring all of us. When Ricou held out his rubber knife, Suzy knocked it out of his hand. Our cameraman, on my instruction, went below the surface with the underwater camera and filmed the whole sequence of "Flipper" disarming and disabling a pirate. It was as if she had known exactly what was on our minds, and so complied with our wishes.

In his book, Antony Alpers made two New Zealand dolphins famous. One was Pelorus Jack who, between 1888 and 1912, acted as a pilot for boats between Wellington and Nelson Harbor, assisting them in avoiding dangerous reefs in Cook Strait. All captains, sailors, and boatmen were acquainted with this incredible dolphin who guided them through the narrows, swimming and leaping ahead of the bow of their ships. For his good work, Pelorus Jack was rewarded by a bullet from a cruel sailor's gun.* Afterward, Wellington mourned its famous dolphin and dedicated a statue to the best pilot Wellington Harbor ever had.

* Today it is a crime in New Zealand to molest or kill a dolphin. In Florida, I persuaded the state senator from Palm Beach to propose a similar law, which has now been enacted.

13   Gentle Ben

I WAS BORN in Hungary at a time when the Carpathian Mountains were still within the borders of the Austro-Hungarian Empire. The only exotic wild animal within our borders was the European brown bear, and most of our childrens' books were about bears. Occasionally a gypsy wandered around town with a dancing bear, and it was a great thrill for us children to see this creature in the flesh.

Bears are very nimble. They have excellent balance. I had seen fantastic bear acts in the Russian circus, among them the most famous of all — a bear ice-hockey team that played against another bear ice-hockey team. Their skating was fabulous.

The reason we like to give human characteristics to bears is because they can walk on their hind legs as humans do. Along with that, bear cubs are cuddly and playful. The funniest animal scene that I ever staged took place in an ice-cream parlor where I let three bear cubs loose. They climbed into the containers and ate all of the ice cream in sight. Their bellies increased to such an extent that it was not easy to pull them out.

Some years later, I joined Dr. Fred White, head of the department of physiology at the UCLA Medical School, in testing the sense of smell of a nine-month-old Kodiak bear. We took him into the Los Angeles National Forest. Professor White had brought a honeycomb with him, and we nailed it to an old tree, picking a spot where the bark had fallen off. We then nailed the bark back over the honeycomb, completely covering it. As soon as the honeycomb was secure and hidden, we went back and let the little bear out of his cage on the road about seven hundred yards away. Then we followed the bear cub. First he simply enjoyed his freedom and loped around. But then some appetizing molecules hit his sensitive nostrils. He immediately got on his hind legs and turned his muzzle in the direction of the honeycomb. Immediately, he broke into a fast gallop, faster than we could follow him. When we caught up with him, he was at the tree.

He could smell the honey, but pinpointing its location might prove to be a problem with the big piece of bark nailed over it. However, we could not fool this honey expert. He was ready to tear the tree apart with his talons. It did not take him long to strip off the bark, and his tongue did not stop lapping up the honey until the last of it was gone. We always get a tremendous laugh from students when we show the film of this scene in a science class.

This olfactory sense is very important for survival because bears are territorial creatures and loners. A male may be a great distance away from a female, but if papa bear could not locate the scent of mama bear, there wouldn't be any baby bears, since the females are in heat only once a year.

The great granddads of all bears were the prehistoric cave bears. They were real giants and many of their descendants are huge even today. Some grizzly bears and Alaskan Kodiak bears can reach a weight up to 2000 pounds. Hunters have shot polar bears that measured seventeen feet and weighed over 2000 pounds. The average American black bear weighs somewhere between 250 and 500 pounds. My average American black bear, Gentle Ben, was seven feet tall and weighed around 700 pounds. He would have made a good basketball player on a black bear team.

The strength of bears is enormous. A grizzly or a Kodiak

bear can kill an ox with one blow of his powerful paw. Luckily, bears are shy creatures and tend to avoid humans. But there are always exceptions. In the United States, the exceptions are the bears in national parks like Yosemite, Yellowstone, Glacier, and Sequoia, where the tourists, although forewarned, often feed the bears and leave garbage behind.

When I was a young man, working as a writer at MGM, the studio made a film in Sequoia National Park, in California. One of the studio employees parked his sedan off the road and left a box of chocolates in it. The car was locked and the windows were rolled up. When he returned to his car in the late afternoon, he could not believe what he saw. There was a gaping hole in the hard top of his car. Obviously, a bear had smelled the chocolates and had climbed onto the top of the car. Then he must have kept jumping with all his weight until the roof of the car caved in. He then had stolen the chocolates and had gone on his merry way.

Recently I visited a wildlife way station in Tujunga Canyon, in southern California, where we collect orphaned and abandoned wild animals. The way station restores them to health and tries to find a good home for them or returns them to the wild. While I was there, a truck arrived from Sequoia National Park. The game guard in charge of bears had brought us a lovely mother bear with two young cubs. They were as sweet as bears can be. The problem was that the mother had figured out how to get into Volkswagens and had made a shambles of some of the tourist cars while she was looking for fruit and sweets. The park had had to pay a total of $30,000 in damages to dozens of tourists. We accepted the bears and agreed to take care of them.

We put the guilty trio in a giant cage. The next morning, the cage was empty. We found the bears on the top of a tree, asleep and snoring. On their very first day, mama bear had figured out how to pick the lock of her new cage. So we lured them down with honey and placed them in a burglar proof cage — or bear proof, I hope. Different animals have different talents.

It was a lucky day for Africa USA, when my friend Ralph Helfer purchased a Wisconsin bear cub named Bruno. Bruno later became the star of *Gentle Ben* the motion picture feature and of the fifty-six episodes of *Gentle Ben* the television series. This little cub did not remain little for long. He grew to giant proportions even for a black bear, making me suspect that Ben was half grizzly. But his nature was not grizzly at all. He was friendly, playful, intelligent, and loving from the first day on. He liked to wrestle with big people, but he never squeezed us, he just liked to hold us. A child or baby or any little animal was safe with Bruno. Now, this does not happen very often. We have worked with bears who were not at all safe. When we turned our backs on them, they would be ready to give us a good shove from behind. So we never turned our backs. Helfer's wife, Tony, and Pat Darby took care of Bruno when he was little, and he appreciated human kindness for the rest of his life. He even became friendly with Flipper. They used to swim together in the hot Florida weather, and we made a film costarring the two buddies, Flipper and Ben.

Ben had a charmed life. I have already mentioned that Ben survived the big flood, when his cage was washed away and broken up. Well, he had another brush with death when a train going through our ranch derailed and the locomotive fell on Ben's cage. It was a miracle that Ben was not killed.

Experience has taught me a lot about animals, and once I get to know their natures, their likes and dislikes, the rest is easy. It takes only common sense to handle them, not any magic. For instance, all bears like sweets, but Ben had a weakness for lemon drops. I always kept lemon drops with me when I played with him. The Eastman Kodak Company was the sponsor of the Gentle Ben TV series, and the advertising agency for Eastman set up a big photographic session on the first day of shooting. Just before the session was to begin, I

Ivan Tors and Gentle Ben (*Bill Ray, Life Magazine,* © *1967 Time, Inc.*)

quietly disappeared behind a car and pushed a lemon drop in my right ear. Then I walked back to the clearing where all the photographers were setting up their cameras. As soon as I arrived, Ben smelled the lemon drop and walked up to me. He stood up on his hind legs and started to lick my ear. It seemed to all present that Ben had come to me to kiss me out of great affection. No one had noticed the lemon drop in my ear, only Ben's enthusiasm. Of course, Ben tried to lap the sweet out, and he soon succeeded. The result of this little scene was some excellent photographs. Even the prestigious *Life* magazine used one of the photographs in a spread about me and my animal friends.

One night, a press conference was arranged for me at the Professional Golfers' Association club in Palm Beach. No one expected me to walk in with my seven-hundred-pound friend. We were a little early, so I walked up to the bar and ordered two drinks, a gin and tonic for myself and a Coca-Cola for Ben. Ben stood at the bar and gulped down the Coke while I was sipping my drink. Suddenly a cocktail waitress came to the bar, without noticing that Ben was standing there. She gave her order to the bartender, then turned to her left and saw this seven-foot bear looming over her. I will never forget that barmaid. She just froze and could not move. I reassured her, but her hands trembled as she carried her loaded tray back to her customers, and half of each drink spilled out.

Now the time arrived for the press conference. I walked into the private conference room with Ben behind me. The room was full of reporters from the various magazines and newspapers. They were all elated when they saw me enter with my leading bear. I sat down in a comfortable armchair, and Ben immediately sat down on the carpet right next to me. He did not move or create any disturbance during the interview. This wasn't really because he was so polite. You see, my pocket was full of lemon drops, and Ben wanted to remain close to the origin of this heavenly scent. He also knew that he would, in due time, receive his reward.

The press was not always friendly. Several months later, I arrived in Miami from Europe and drove to the Ivan Tors Studios. There were lots of people who looked like strangers to me milling around the sound stages. When I got to my office, my assistants informed me that there was a news reporters' convention in Miami Beach, and about a hundred reporters were waiting for an interview with me. I was flattered by this evidence of my popularity, although I had no inkling what the interview was to be about since I had not read an American newspaper for days. My assistants ushered the reporters into one of our sound stages, and I got up on a table. My soundman gave me a microphone, and I told the press that they could ask me any questions they wished. In the next few minutes I realized what had happened in the United States while I was in Europe. A tragedy involving bears had occurred in one of our national parks.

The story, as I remember it, was that two young women who were camping at night in the open in Glacier National Park, were attacked in their sleeping bags by bears, carried away, and killed. The press asked me pointblank how I dared to present a television series glorifying the gentleness of bears while such vicious attacks were taking place.

I faced a tough situation, and I knew I had to keep my cool and come up with an intelligent answer. My mind was fired up. When do animals behave strangely and violently and out of character? Bears are basically shy, except in national parks. Then I remembered a time when one of my best male lions went absolutely berserk when a young woman approached his cage. He drove himself into a frenzy because he could not break through the bars of his cage, and in his frustration he attacked the large wooden box he usually slept in and bit the box into smithereens, filling his mouth with splinters. Ralph Helfer had to tranquilize him with a hypodermic gun, and while he was asleep, we removed around thirty splinters from his mouth. Later I learned that the woman was having her period, and the scent caused the lion's unreasonable excitement.

Thinking of this, I answered my inquisitors. "Gentlemen, bears have an incredible sense of smell. This is the only way they can locate a mate at great distances. I just heard about this unfortunate incident, but I would bet my bottom dollar that the savaged women had been having their periods."

It was an educated guess but it was also the correct answer. Two weeks later, the investigation instituted by the park had established that both young tourists were menstruating at the time this savagery occurred.

But this episode should be a lesson to us. Wild animals are not safe with people. Not because they are necessarily aggressive, but because they are equipped with lethal weapons and they are big. Very few of them are vicious. I am repeating myself, but I want to say again that a five-hundred-pound lion can kill you by jumping on you simply to express his love and joy. Only experts should handle wild animals and poisonous snakes or swim among sharks, killer whales, and other potentially lethal creatures.

I have been lucky. I have never been hurt by a wild animal, but I know many who have — among them some of the best experts. If something scares a tame giraffe — and a giraffe can kick four ways at the same time — he can maim you in one second while you are leading him by a halter to a stable.

A good example of the unsuspected danger that may develop from even the most gentle creatures is the story of a dolphin. Dr. Lilly and I never found a dolphin that showed aggressive tendencies after capture, yet he had heard about a dolphin in an aquarium that was ready to bite off your hand when you touched the water. The dolphin soon died, and the autopsy proved that she had had a broken neck. The fisherman who had caught the dolphin had broken her neck while lifting her into his boat. The poor creature must have been in agony all during the time that she was in the aquarium.

About twenty years ago, there occurred the first case of a lion attacking a tourist in the Serengeti. When the game warden shot the offending lion, he found a giant tumor on its right shoulder. The creature had been in pain and could hunt for nothing but slow-moving humans.

There are always dangerous exceptions to the rules, and when you decide to live among wild animals or tame wild animals, no one hands you an insurance policy. It has been my way of life to take chances. It is the choice of my sons to take chances. We love Africa, we love animals, and facing danger is the price we pay — willingly.

Bears living in regions of cold winters cannot survive in the open when snow covers the earth. After December, there isn't enough food available above the ground, so the bear goes underground. During the summer and autumn, bears eat constantly so as to accumulate enough fat in their huge bodies to sustain them through the tough winter. Usually, they will find a comfortable cave or a hollow tree trunk where, with reduced metabolism, they can survive until the first buds break through the icy cover.

In this state of half-sleep, the female will give birth to her young — most often, to two. The newborn bears are hairless and weigh hardly a pound. But by the time spring arrives, the cubs are able to follow their now skinny mother as she sets out to fatten herself up for another year. The female bear is a disciplinarian, and when the cubs take chances that may endanger them, mama bear will punish them by cuffing the guilty parties. She is an excellent mother, but when the cubs she loves so much reach a certain age, she will decide that the time has come for them to fend for themselves, to survive on their own. When the biological clock tells her that the time has come, she chases her beloved cubs away. Bears need a lot of territory to survive. Three adults could not live on the same land. The half-grown cubs must find their own pieces of land. The law of survival has orchestrated a symphony for the bear: first movement, mating; second movement, hibernating; third movement, bringing up cubs; fourth movement, making cubs independent. This is nature's way.

My life in the wild has proved to me again and again that nature works through very precise rules. In certain species, only those who cooperate will survive. Among the loners, like the bears, the mother must let go of her cubs when the time has arrived. Among the ungulates, only the strongest bulls father offspring. Even among the humanlike baboons, only the dominant male will beget children. Among lions, the unhealthy do not survive the first six months of life. Among the elephants, nature demands a constant loving care for the young.

Those who wander away from the herd are easy victims for jackals or hyenas. The single gazelle will be picked up by the cheetah, and the slowest impala will be dragged into the water by the crocodile. Nature tries to improve the gene pool of each species. Only we humans go against nature's laws. We try to keep everybody alive, even those whose bad seeds may endanger our species. We cure the nomads of cholera and then infect them with tuberculosis. We eliminate malaria in the tropics and introduce venereal diseases there. People with good minds practice birth control; those with feeble minds propagate extensively. Unlike the bear, we are permissive with our offspring. The baboons have a rank order they abide by, while we repeatedly revolt against order.

I believe that Darwin was exceptionally perceptive to realize that there is order in nature and that the road to our self-destruction very well could be an utter disregard for what nature tries to tell us. Nature talks to us all the time, but mankind refuses to listen. It is the oldest truth of all that, in this whole universe, only men and a few insects wage war against each other.

14   Clarence and His Kind

I WOULD LIKE to take you back, twelve years before my experience with the lion in the Serengeti, to when I had a very
different meeting with a lion — in Soledad Canyon in southern
California, on our newly founded animal farm, Africa USA.
Ralph Helfer, my partner and the manager of the farm, introduced me to a strange-looking lion cub and suggested that
we give this young lion away because he had problems with
his vision — the young lion was completely cross-eyed.

"Did you say we should give this cub away?" I asked Ralph
incredulously. He nodded. I shook my head. "No, Ralph, I've
never seen a cross-eyed lion, and neither has the rest of the
world. I made Flipper famous and I'll make Clarence famous."

Ralph looked at me strangely. "His name is Freddie. I've already named him."

"Sorry, Ralph," I said. "His name is now Clarence. It's a fun-
nier name, and he is a funny lion." The future star of *Daktari,*
thus rebaptized by me, was to become for seven years the most
beloved lion in the civilized world and a winner of the Patsy
Award, which is given to great animal performers.

Clarence was an unusual creature, without any instinct of
aggression. He was a lover, not a fighter. As he grew up, we
lavished affection on him, and eventually he became one of the
most beautiful full-maned lions I had ever set eyes on. His fur

Clarence as a baby (*Metro-Goldwyn-Mayer*)

was golden brown and silky; his temperament was even and friendly. He was one of the few lions that tolerated children. Nor did he mind Judy, the chimp, sitting on his back or pulling his tail. Clarence won everyone's heart. He was the Shirley Temple of the lion world.

One day, I parked my station wagon close to Clarence's enclosure and took him for a walk. When he saw my car, he wanted to jump into the back — which was his usual place — but the back door was closed, and he banged his head against it. It was then I realized that his eyesight had become worse. The next day, I telephoned Dr. Leonard Apt at the Jules Stein Eye Institute at the University of California at Los Angeles. Dr. Apt specializes in restoring the vision of cross-eyed children, and I asked him whether he would drive the fifty miles to examine my cross-eyed lion. Since he doesn't often get an opportunity to examine lions, he accepted the challenge, perhaps with some apprehension. Nevertheless, he arrived on a Sunday with his little black bag equipped with various complicated, sophisticated instruments.

I led the patient to the doctor on a leash, and Dr. Apt proceeded to examine Clarence without any trepidation. My respect for Dr. Apt increased because it was obvious that he cared about his patient first, and his own safety after that. Clarence was not the best patient in the world; in fact, he was a little impatient, and at one point, he jumped over Dr. Apt's head. The doctor, remaining unruffled, continued looking into Clarence's eyes with his instruments until he was ready to give his diagnosis. An operation would not improve the vision, it would only cause unnecessary hardship. He patted his five-hundred-pound patient on the back and never sent us a bill.

Two years later, I arrived in New York from London and checked into the Plaza Hotel. The hotel was jammed because an international eye convention was taking place there, and all the top eye specialists of the world were present, including Dr. Apt. We stepped into the elevator together and Dr. Apt inquired, "Ivan, how is your cross-eyed lion?" The other doctors looked at us strangely, but Apt continued. "You know, it's time for another examination."

"Might contact lenses be the answer for him?" I asked.

Leonard liked the idea. "Contact lenses for your lion? Not bad."

The elevator reached my floor and I got out. I had the feeling that Dr. Apt was being scrutinized of his fellow scientists because, after all, who ever heard of a cross-eyed lion?

I loved Clarence. I did not think of him as a lion. To me, he was like a cuddly stuffed toy, but often full of surprises. And one of them happened when we started to film our first *Daktari* episode early one morning. We forgot to tell Clarence that, before the camera rolls, the assistant claps two boards together for the soundman. The camera was in position. Clarence was in position. The director said the magic words, "Roll it!" The assistant clapped the slate. The sudden noise scared Clarence.

He jumped twenty feet over the camera crew and disappeared up the mountain. It took us an hour and a half, following lion spoors, to find him, and then we had to reassure him so he would let us bring him back to the set.

Helfer was the best lion man in the business, and I learned a great deal from him about taming, treating, and handling lions. I learned that a lion's muscle strength will exceed a man's in a four-to-one ratio. This means that a 400-pound lion has the muscle power of 1600 pounds of human strength. In turn, this means that eight people cannot restrain or handle a lion when he does not want to be handled. I learned that lions are affectionate creatures who like to touch each other and lick each other's fur. The touch of humans rubbing their backs is also very pleasurable to them. So we established a regimen with our thirty lions, taking them for a walk each day, rubbing them, brushing them, and even nuzzling their young. The result was that these lions were tame but not circus trained, and they desired our touch more than the food we gave them. When we

Clarence in specs (*Metro-Goldwyn-Mayer*)

approached their enclosures, they lined up next to the fence to be rubbed and touched. I maintain that there is no love without touching. And this belief has become part of my handling of both animals and humans, children and adults. It has worked well for me.

There is something about lions that I find unique among earth creatures. In the wild, they take it for granted that all belongs to them. They have no superiors. I once watched a lion resting in the path of an approaching herd of elephants. The elephants came with deliberate speed. The first few were giants who could rub a 450-pound lion into the dust. The lion did not move but kept resting until the last moment. When the lead elephant was upon him, he stood up slowly, with dignity, and walked in front of them as though he were leading their column.

Another time, I heard from a traveler that, in Mozambique, a pride of lions had moved into a housing project near Gorongoza. I sent a camera crew to photograph them. About six two-story, frame houses had been built on a road in the wilderness for some mining surveyors, but the summer rains had flooded the area, and the human inhabitants had moved out. When they returned, each house was occupied by a family of lions who had expropriated the clean shady buildings. They liked them more than the thorn bushes that are their natural habitat. When we got there, the lions were sunning themselves on the roofs or walking up and down the narrow staircases. The young ones had a great deal of fun rolling down the stairs and peering through the windows. It was a true lion city, and our presence did not seem to excite them at all or make them aggressive.

What I like about lions in nature is, while they have the power to kill and kill fast, they kill only to eat. The lonely traveler is safe from them during the day, but at night, when they are more active, lions are a little more dangerous. A pride once chased my friend Dr. Murray Watson up a tree, where he was forced to stay until daylight. On the other hand, when I once

Clarence in the office (*Bill Ray, Life Magazine,* © *1967 Time, Inc.*)

dug myself a shelter for the night on a river bank, I awakened in the morning to find that four lions had rested in the bush next to me without ever bothering me.

One should not take a lion out of nature and later attempt to return him to it. The book and film *Born Free* were about this problem. It was proved again to us in Zululand by a strange incident in the life of my friend Nick Steele. Nick was Ian Player's right-hand man, at that time, as a game guard. (Later he became the game warden of the whole territory.) Nick, who did not like to live among people, stayed in a small cottage on the other side of the Umfolozi River. Every single night when he drove home to his pretty wife, Nola, and their newborn baby, he parked his Land-Rover on the left bank of the river and swam across the crocodile-infested, black river. When I asked him whether he was not being foolish to take such chances, he shrugged his shoulders, explaining to me that crocodiles are slow learners and that he fools the crocs by swimming across at a different spot every night. I don't know whether he was right or wrong, but Nick is still strong and healthy.

One night, Nick returned home as usual after his swim across the river. He entered his house, kissed his wife and baby, dried himself off, then sat down to dinner. Night fell, and the family was about to retire when they heard a loud commotion in their garden. Nick flashed a light through the window and saw his goats and chickens running around, scared, inside the picket fence. A full-grown lion was in the garden. Strangely, the lion did not attack any of the easy prey or even get excited. The lion was determined to enter the house. He jumped against the door, but the door did not give. He kept clawing at it. Nick and Nola were terrified, especially because Nick had never before witnessed such lion behavior. He loaded his gun just in time. When the lion came sailing through the window, shattering the glass, Nick had no choice. He had to kill the lion with one shot.

The lookout (*Metro-Goldwyn-Mayer*)

The mystery of the housebreaking lion was explained only much later. The lion had been a circus animal. After the circus had gone bankrupt, a well-to-do animal lover had purchased the lion, then set it free in the game reserve without consulting an expert. The fact of the matter was that the lion, born in captivity, was scared to death in nature and especially of the dark. When he spotted the lights in Nick's window, he had rushed there for refuge, to be safe with humans. His intention was not to kill but to be protected by man. Nick, who is an ardent conservationist, was heartbroken by the adventure. However, with his wife and baby in the room, he had had no other choice.

Just recently I heard that some young Californian nature lovers purchased a lion in order to send it to Africa, to let it go free. I hope they will seek some professional advice.

15   In Defense of the Shark

SHARKS ARE UNIQUE CREATURES. They are older than dinosaurs and they were threats to other creatures in the sea more than three hundred million years ago. There are as many sharks in the sea today as there ever were, but we find more of them in tropical waters than in icy cold seas. Man has an inherent fear of the shark, the snake, and the crocodile. It took me a long time to lose this fear.

Hungary is a landlocked country quite devoid of sharks, but when I was ten years old, my family and I spent our summer vacation on the shore of the Adriatic Sea. It was here for the first time that I heard a lot of talk about man-eating sharks, and I was warned not to venture too far out in the sea. The bathers talked about a swimmer whose leg had been cut off by a shark some twenty years before, and the memory of that single attack was enough to make most of the bathers swim scared and stay away from the deep. Later on, although I crossed the Atlantic, cruised around the Mediterranean, visited the Florida coast many times, and spent a great deal of time on the Pacific shores, during the first thirty-five years of my life I never saw a shark or a shark fin in any of these waters.

I was twenty-four years old when I moved to California and saw the Pacific Ocean for the first time. It was love at first sight, and I tried to be on the beach as often as my unemployed status would allow, and that was plenty. The very first time I swam in the Pacific, when I was about three hundred yards offshore, something big and black popped up next to me in the waves. It was heart attack time. I was sure it was a shark. On the shore, my dog kept barking fiercely as I tried to swim, at top speed, away from the black thing. Suddenly it overtook me, popped up next to my head — and barked.

This is how I met my first sea lion. It was a great relief. I scrambled to the shore and watched the sea lion playing in the waves while my dog kept up his clamor.

After that time, I became involved in making underwater films. Between 1955 and 1975, I filmed over three hundred fifty underwater television episodes and ten features with underwater backgrounds. In all this time, no one in my crew was ever bothered by a shark. When I filmed the MGM picture *Underwater Warriors*, a true history of the American frogmen, I asked Commander Fane, the commander of the underwater demolition team, whether any of his frogmen had been attacked by a shark. His answer was a qualified no. The qualification was that the tip of the rubber fin of one of his swimmers was once bitten off by a shark, but the swimmer was left unharmed.

From that time on, I dedicated myself to the idea of appraising the reality or unreality of shark danger. After twenty-two years of study, I have come to the following conclusion: Yes, there is a danger that a swimmer can be hit by a shark. The chances are about the same as being hit by a yellow Rolls-Royce.

Then why have certain people been attacked by sharks? The answer is that those people were not attacked by sharks but by certain sharks. To demonstrate this, I can offer an example. In July 1916, five swimmers were savaged at different times off the New Jersey coast. Later, a big shark was caught and killed, and in its belly some remnants of all victims were found. The

Captain Fane with a white-tipped shark, near Eniwetok (*Metro-Goldwyn-Mayer*)

guilty party was a single nine-foot white shark. Nothing like this happened again on the Jersey coast until 1960, when another shark bit three people — but not fatally.

In 1958, I made my first shark documentary at the Marshall Islands. Commander Fane took my filming unit where there were always plenty of sharks. It was close to shore, and the sewage from a Navy stockyard and butcher shop seeped into the crystal clear lagoon, inviting all the neighborhood sharks.

I did not want to endanger any of my divers or camera crew, so we constructed a shark cage, which we lowered from our work boat into the lagoon, with our divers and camera crew inside the cage. Then we speared an eighty-pound grouper and left the bleeding fish on the bottom of the lagoon, close to our cage. Suddenly a nine-foot mako shark appeared and sliced the big fish in two with one vicious bite — and then devoured it with great appetite. Even now, looking at the film is scary. It proves the possibility of a nine-foot shark slicing a human in two just as easily. The only difference is that fish are on the menu of a shark, and humans are not. When Commander Fane and his frogmen swam out of the cage, toward the same shark, the shark did not seem to be bothered, and it took only slight interest. It circled the commander twice, then swam away.

At that time, this behavior was a surprise to me. Now I know why. The speared fish was bleeding, exciting the olfactory organ of the shark and guiding it to the victim. The grouper, in its death struggle, sent out low-frequency vibrations, another invitation to a shark's guidance system. The cut on the speared fish changed the electric circuitry around the dying fish, and this change activated certain electric receptors of the shark's, which then also acted as direction finders. Besides all this, the shape and form of a fish was familiar and inviting to the shark, while the human form was not. When the human form accidentally takes on a shape or pattern that confuses the shark and falls in line with the feeding patterns of the shark, then shark attacks will occur.

To explain this feeding pattern is quite simple. I spent a great deal of time in the Bahamas, and I did not hear of any shark attacks occurring there. When we caught some tiger sharks, their bellies were full of lobsters. I guess the sharks in the Bahamas eat only lobsters. So do I, when I'm there. People do not look like lobsters, so we do not fall into the sharks' feeding pattern around those waters.

On the other hand, in Queensland, Australia, the big sharks love to feed on slowmoving turtles. Their giant jaws can bite through the toughest turtle shells. I was in Brisbane when a young surfer sat on his surfboard with his feet hanging into the water. A shark, observing this shape from below, could easily mistake it for the shape of a turtle. A shark did just that and bit off the foot of the young man. This was a case when a human fell into the feeding pattern of the Great Barrier Reef shark.

Sharks cannot turn as fast as other fish, so a single fish can escape attack by a shark. A school of fish is a different story. The scales will reflect the sunlight, and the shark will hit the school. By the law of averages, he is bound to catch one of the thousands of these fishes traveling together. Now, when we splash on the surface of the water, we create bubbles. The sunlight reflected off the bubbles looks the same as sunlight glinting off small fish. When Commander Fane's frogman swam, the tip of his fins created the same kind of bubbles. It is very likely that the shark attacked the bubbles and not the man.

Commander Fane told me again and again, if you meet a shark, don't panic. Swim toward the shark and not away. Fish swim away from sharks. When you move toward the shark, you do not fit the shark's feeding pattern. A man is big and unknown to the shark, and the shark's very primitive nervous system cannot quickly sort out what it is he faces. Most of the time, the shark will then swim away. Even when a big, hungry shark spots a man, the shark may circle him for twenty to thirty minutes before deciding on an attack, and that gives the swimmer enough time to get out of the dangerous waters.

Some divers become so overconfident with sharks, that they occasionally pay an expensive price. A case in point was a Navy diver who was placing a seismic device on the ocean floor at Guam. A medium-sized shark circled him for thirty minutes while he paid no attention. Finally, the shark hit him in the shoulder and took out a chunk. The Navy diver survived, but we all earned the lesson never to underestimate the chance of an attack, even if it may not happen frequently.

Now, the picture changes completely when sharks are in a feeding frenzy. Once they have tasted food, their nervous system is excited. They will keep hitting the same target. For instance, if six fishermen go spear fishing together and one spears a fish, the scent of blood and the vibration of the speared fish hanging on the belt of the diver may attract a shark. The shark will first hit the fish on the belt, and, in taking the fish, he may take a piece of the man. Once he has attacked this man, the shark will disregard all others and will keep coming back to attack the same bleeding man. The diver can be carried to safety by his buddies who will be quite safe from attack since the shark has only one target in mind.

One day, for our filming purposes, we baited a coral reef with chunks of fish. The scent brought in about twelve big sharks. The hungry sharks worked themselves up to an incredible feeding frenzy. They stole chunks from each other, and when one of the fat sharks accidentally got wedged in between two reefs of coral, twisting and twisting to get free, the rest of the sharks attacked and devoured it in their furor. Sharks are often cannibalistic.

On the other hand, there is no predicting. Once in the Bahamas, when we needed a shark for filming, we baited a hook with a barracuda and let it float about seventy-five feet under our diving boat. Sharks like the taste of barracuda. Willie Meyers, exfrogman and world-famous diver, and my son Steve dove down to see whether our bait had lured in any big ones. They were up again soon, both very excited because they had seen a seventeen-foot tiger shark circling our bait. This was the second largest specimen ever sighted. My camera crew jumped into the water to photograph the big one. When the shark spotted my crew, it turned tail and swam away. We could get no closer than two hundred feet, which is too far for good photographs. Nevertheless, tiger sharks are considered man-eaters by many. My experience leads me to disagree.

Another time, we were filming on a wreck when another man-eater, a scary-looking hammerhead shark, suddenly appeared in front of our cameras at a time when we did not need any sharks. He kept cruising around us and getting in our way. So Big John, our master diver, and Courtney Brown, another great diver, grabbed the big hammerhead, one from the left side, the other from the right, and swim-carried him out of the scene. The shark did not show any resistance and accepted the eviction good-naturedly.

One day we were filming underwater at Lyford Key in the

Big John handling a shark in the Bahamas (*Photo by Don Renn*)

Bahamas for the TV series *Aquanaut*. We had a female diver in the scene, playing the part of an archaeologist who finds an ancient wreck full of antique vases, or amphorae. As she went through her underwater acting, a ten-foot shark appeared from nowhere and swam toward her. She did not lose her nerve, however. She picked up an amphora and hit the shark right on the nose with the big vase. The shark therefore understood that she did not want to make its acquaintance, so it turned around and swam toward my cameraman Lamar Boren, who pushed his 300-pound underwater camera at the shark's nose to shoo it away. Then the shark swam toward Courtney Brown. Courtney reached for his diving knife and hit the shark with the knife handle, right on the tip of the nose. The shark knew by now that he was not welcome and swam away without a fuss. A reporter from *Life* magazine, who was observing with me underwater, did not want to believe his eyes. Yet it was all in a day's work for our underwater crews to live in peaceful coexistence with these big sharks.

There are more than two hundred species of sharks, which are very unusual fish. Instead of scales, sharks have a tough skin covered with denticles, sharp teethlike projections. Instead of bone, the shark's skeleton is made of cartilage. Fish have air bladders to keep them afloat. Sharks do not have these organs, so, in order to breath and stay afloat, they are forced to keep moving all the time. Shallow water sharks, such as sand sharks and nurse sharks, position themselves on the bottom, at strategic places, where the underwater current will sufficiently oxygenate them.

The deep water cruising sharks are called pelagic sharks and thus the so-called man-eaters — such as the great white shark, tiger shark, Greenland shark, and mako shark — are all pelagic. The largest, but now-extinct species of shark, which was similar to the great white shark, grew to sizes of eighty feet or longer, the size of a good-sized whale.

The largest shark living today is the whale shark, which may grow to sizes between twenty-five and forty-five feet in length.

Interestingly, this largest species of all is the least dangerous, because the whale shark is not a flesh eater. Its diet is plankton, and it swims with its giant mouth half open, filtering out the plankton. In fact, the feeding habits of the two largest shark specimens, the whale shark and the basking shark, are similar to the feeding habits of the baleen whales.

My friend Ben Cropp, the Australian shark expert and shark photographer, once took excellent pictures of this whale-sized giant while his wife, Eva, and one of his diving buddies held onto the fin. The shark probably did not feel the weight or presence of a tiny human since the whale shark's skin is reportedly four inches thick — so thick that it is almost impossible to strike a harpoon through it. The blade of a sharp knife will break off on contact. But why should anyone harm a harmless shark?!

The basking shark is equally harmless and somewhat smaller than the whale shark. A friend of mine was cruising with his small motorboat in Puget Sound, when he looked over his shoulder and realized that he was not alone. He was being followed by a monster of a shark with its mouth half open, looking as if he were ready to swallow my friend's Boston Whaler. He soon realized, however, that the creature enjoyed inhaling his exhaust fumes and that was why it was playing follow the leader.

It is interesting to note that these giants are most efficient biological machines. Our oceans are full of plankton, and metabolizing plankton produces ten times more calories than eating the fish that feed on plankton. Ten pounds of plankton will produce only one pound of fish, so these giant creatures, like the great baleen whales, are the best conservationists.

The most feared carnivorous shark is the great white shark made immortal by *Jaws*. (I liked the film, though I consider it less a film about sharks than a good science-fiction horror movie.) Ben Cropp has photographed great white sharks for me many times, and he has never been molested by the "white pointer," as they are called in Australia. It is true that, because of its size and excellent teeth, a great white shark could consume a man easily, but there have been very few incidents of a great white actually attacking a swimmer. In my studies of shark attacks in Australia, I found that 90 percent of those attacks (and there were not very many) had been directed against spear fishermen. There were a few exceptions, such as an incident when a lady was bitten on a beach in shallow water. I suspect that she stepped on the shark. The underwater photographers I interviewed had never been attacked, and scuba divers seldom. People who hunted fish with spears were the ones who suffered occasional shark attacks, but even these were rare.

Some of my friends once spent a million dollars making a film to prove the viciousness of the great white shark. They cruised around the world, lowering shark cages and confronting great white sharks, but the only time they succeeded in photographing attacks was when they baited the giants by throwing dead horses and sheep into the ocean, which produced feeding frenzy. Thus, the whole world would be able to see how cruel the sharks were. But, to look at it objectively, the cruelty of the photographers was what succeeded in changing some peaceful white sharks into cruel, bloodthirsty beasts. I must ask the question, "Who started it?"

Unfortunately, during World War II, many shipwrecked sailors and survivors of airplane crashes were eaten by sharks. Why? When I was in the Air Force in World War II, we received a booklet instructing us on what to do in case we had to ditch our planes and ended up in the drink. The first piece of advice was, "Kick and Splash!" That was the worst advice! Kicking causes shark-attracting low-frequency vibrations, and the ditching of the plane itself would have already sent out sound signals alerting the sharks. Also, the blood of someone wounded would send out olfactory signals, and soon the sharks would be there. If the survivors were not picked up by lifeboats soon, the time would arrive for a feeding frenzy. In defense of the shark, it is only fair to point out that man's cruelty in a bloody war at sea is what triggers the cruelty of sharks.

This propensity is not unique to sharks. Lions normally are not man-eaters but, after the Boer War in South Africa, there were so many dead bodies lying around that scavenging lions acquired a taste for easy meals and thus got used to the taste of human flesh. After the war, there remained a few man-eating lions, but when they had been shot, the rest returned to their normal diet of zebra, antelope, and warthog.

Most sharks are not very pretty. They are equipped with seven or more rows of razor-sharp teeth. By sliding their jaws, they can use them as a hacksaw. If sharks lose their front teeth while biting into steel or a harpoon, the next row will move up as immediate replacement. In a feeding frenzy, they will swallow anything. Shackles, chains, shoes, a missionary's stiff collar, beer bottles, and sundry other items found in sharks' bellies have been photographed by Commander Fane.

In December 1965, I received a call from Cubby Broccoli, the producer of the James Bond films. He asked me whether I could help him with his new picture *Thunderball*. "What do you need?" I asked him. He needed seven tiger sharks on March 15 in Nassau. "You'll have them," I promised.

I rented a shark-catching boat and put Ricou Browning in charge. The boat was under the command of Captain Hansen who collects specimens for Miami's Seaquarium. There was a pool on the deck, and with a winch we could hoist a big shark onto the deck and into the saltwater pool, where it could survive. We anchored the boat a hundred yards off Lyford Key, (where the millionaires live) and, every night, we threw out lines baited with barracuda. Every morning, we winched in fair-sized tiger sharks. This operation proved that the sea off the resort was teeming with tiger sharks, and yet I have never heard that anyone was ever harmed by a shark at Lyford Key. On March 15, we sailed to a dock at Emerald Beach and, with the help of a crane, unloaded seven tiger sharks into a specially built saltwater swimming pool. The sharks were sluggish because not enough oxygen had passed through their gills in the pool. So we all jumped into the water with the sharks and walked them. Each of us pushed a shark at a fast pace through the water to oxygenate them and make them more lively.

None of the sharks showed any bad temper or aggression while we worked with them. Cubby saw me walking a shark, and he was too good a showman to let it go. On the afternoon when Sean Connery arrived, Cubby suggested a new scene in which 007 would swim across the pool among the sharks. Sean was not too happy with the suggestion. Cubby suddenly pointed at me. "Look at this old man. If he can do it, certainly you can do it." So, at Cubby's request, I swam among the sharks, and poor Sean was shamed into doing the same, a job usually performed only by a stuntman for a lot of money. I think Connery had a lot of guts to accept that challenge. After all, he did not have the experience or the conditioning of an underwater crew man.

To make a long story short, the underwater footage photographed by Lamar Boren, Jordan Klein's fantastic gadgets, and Ricou's incredible direction all created a sensation. Every time our footage was projected for the studio executives, they asked us to do more and more. Finally we captured about forty-eight sharks. We tied tiger sharks to coral reefs with invisible nylon lines, then filmed them from helicopters. We pushed a shark through the cockpit of a ditching bomber. We had more shark contact in that one film than any one had ever experienced before.

Nevertheless, we had a few mishaps. A spear gun accidentally went off and speared Ricou, and the accident put him in the hospital for a day or two. Courtney had his air hose snagged, and he passed out. Because his part demanded that he "pass out," we admired his acting while he actually nearly drowned. Luckily, we noticed his distress in time and resuscitated him instantly.

Thus, we had our problems, but never with sharks. We enjoyed the great challenge the James Bond film afforded us, and when the film received an Oscar for special underwater effects, we were all very proud. After the six-million-dollar film had grossed sixty-five million dollars in the theaters, Cubby and United Artists were equally proud. The zoological experience — including capturing almost fifty tiger sharks without killing them, handling them with bare hands, swimming among them, and walking them in a pool — all had taken place without a scratch inflicted by a shark.

Sharks are dangerous, but they are not monsters. To live in fear of sharks and not enjoy the ocean is just as stupid as not to take a shower for fear that one may slip in the bathroom and bang one's head. There are dangers in the oceans from far smaller creatures. Sea snakes, for example, have a venom that can kill a swimmer. Luckily they are not aggressive. The scorpion fish looks beautiful with its colorful quills, but it contains cobra venom. The Portuguese man-of-war can sting you, and, if you are allergic, you can be very badly affected. You can step on a sea urchin, get a shock from an electric ray, or be bitten by a moray eel when you reach into a hole for a lobster. All outdoor activities have some hidden dangers. Lightning can strike you, killer bees can finish you off, you can step on a rattle snake while walking barefoot, and a yellow Rolls-Royce may hit you at midnight if you are not careful.

I learned in nature that fear is the real danger because it weakens you. There is some risk in everything — in birth, love, marriage. And life always ends with death. A healthy person must condition himself to accept life as it is. We must acquire a positive philosophy, faith, and a sense of humor, or life will not be worth living.

To return to sharks — the United States has a hell of a long coastline, with millions of bathers enjoying it. In Los Angeles alone, on warm weekends, there are countless swimmers. In forty-four years, only eighty-five shark attacks were recorded on our coastlines, and perhaps fifteen of them were fatal. That is one fatality every three years. Lightning kills more than thirty people a year. Tornados kill hundreds, hurricanes thousands, cars maim millions, and still we fear the shark more than any other disaster.

In defense of the shark, I'll say that I hope one day we'll be able to learn some of the shark's secrets. Sharks do not get infections, cancer, or many of the other diseases that humans, mammals, and other fish and creatures contract. They seem to have many natural immunities. I've seen sharks with hooks or harpoons imbedded in their heads or mouths, and still there was no sign of infection or tissue deterioration. Sharks are protected in mysterious ways. Is it the extra-large liver with a very high vitamin content? We do not know the full answer to that, although Dr. Linus Pauling believes that a high dosage of vitamins will prevent many diseases, and other Nobel Prize winners agree with him. Maybe we should work with sharks rather than laboratory mice. No creature is useless in nature, and so the man-eaters may one day save our lives.

I have learned not to fear sharks. We do not have to love them, but neither do we have to eliminate them. Garbage disposals aren't pretty, but they do serve a purpose, as does the shark.

So support your neighborhood shark!

16 Namu

IN THE SUMMER of 1966 I arrived in London from Kenya on a glorious Sunday morning, but my mood did not stay glorious long. At a newsstand I read the headline NAMU, THE KILLER WHALE IS DEAD. I did not want to believe it, but reading the paper I learned that my good friend Namu, in Seattle Harbor, had become entangled in the net of his enclosure and had drowned.

I knew why he had died. He loved to be with us in Rich Cove, on the other side of Puget Sound, where he had ample water and many friends and where we filmed our picture *Namu, the Killer Whale*. This is the place where we tried to learn how to communicate with each other, came to respect each other, and played with each other — and then suddenly it was over. The filming was finished. I took off for Africa, and my friend Ted Griffin could not renew our lease on the cove. So Namu was transferred to small quarters in Seattle.

My immediate feeling upon reading the headline was that Namu had tried to return to us at Rich Cove and, in his effort, had become hopelessly entangled. In the dark of the night, no one had noticed his plight. Being an air-breathing mammal, a whale can stay underwater for a certain period of time only. This period is estimated to be somewhere between ten minutes and a half hour. After that, if his blowhole cannot reach the surface of the sea, his fate is sealed.

Namu provided an incredible experience in my life, one that changed many of my convictions about animal nature and helped me develop the new philosophy that I now live by.

My interest in killer whales started in 1955 when a sportsman visited me in my offices and asked me to join him in capturing the first killer whale. At that time, I knew very little about killer whales. My visitor was an experienced and enthusiastic sport-fisherman who had witnessed a scene at Point Lobos in northern California that he said he would never forget.

The scene he described was strictly out of a horror movie. Killer whales at that time were reputed to be the most vicious attackers in the oceans. Their size was estimated somewhere between twenty and twenty-five feet in length, their weight up to twelve thousand pounds. Their dorsal fins cut through the water like black knives. The dorsal fins of the bulls stand out six feet above the water line, and although they are not giants among whales, even the largest of the other whales are afraid of them because in a group the killers may attack sixty-foot whales, bite out their tongues, eat their lips, and destroy them with vicious savagery. I had heard all this before, but this eyewitness related a different kind of incident.

Where he fished at Point Lobos, in the Monterey area, there are many seal islands. The killer whales usually circle these islands, and the scared seals and sea lions take refuge on the rocks. When they are all out of the water in comparative safety, the killer whale jumps high out of the water and then, turning on its side, strikes the water with its giant fin. The slap of the fin hitting the water sounds like an exploding cannon. The noise terrifies the seals, and their instinctive reflex is to jump into the sea for safety. This is what the killer whale is really after. Now it picks off the smaller seals or the sea lions and throws them high up in the air, playing with them for a while before biting them in two and swallowing them. My visitor had witnessed such a blood bath, one worse than a nightmare. This is how he came to ask me if I would be interested in helping him capture a killer whale.

Being a born adventurer, I said yes, and we decided to design a harpoon containing curare, which would temporarily paralyze the killer whale so we could capture the monster. This was long before hypodermic guns were used on animals. We tried it without success. The harpoon did not carry farther than twenty-five feet, and it was impossible to approach a killer whale that close. The result of my interest, however, was some good filming by Ron Church, who captured a scene of a bull killer whale jumping around small islands and scaring his victims into the water. We got these shots at the islands Guadalupe and Saint Benito off the Baja California coast. In this area, killer whales sometimes attack the migrating fifty-five-foot gray whales and panic the big grays by their mere presence. So my first impression of killer whales was that they are the most vicious creatures nature has created and all of them should be exterminated.

Later, I made a *Sea Hunt* episode about killer whales, using Ron's film depicting the cruelty of the wild creature of the sea. It brought out some little known facts about killer whale capacity — as in the incident when a killer, harpooned from a whaling ship, proved to have the remnants of thirteen dolphins and fourteen seal carcasses in its stomach.

When we hear such stories we get scared. But when we have chicken livers for lunch, we are likely to forget that about six innocent chickens were killed to provide one simple meal. All living things are biological machines and need calories as fuel. An elephant, being a herbivore, may eat eight hundred pounds of fiber a day. A killer whale of the same size, being a meat and fish eater, must also consume comparable amounts of calories to keep itself alive. It took me a few years of growing up before I accepted that creatures besides me are allowed to eat too.

My mind was changed about killer whales in June of 1965. I

was filming *Flipper* in Florida, and my wife and children were with me at the Key Biscayne Hotel, when the news came onto my television screen that a large bull killer whale was snagged in a giant net lost by a fishing boat in a storm off the Canadian coast near a fishing village called Namu. Ted Griffin, the young and able owner of the Seattle Aquarium, immediately flew up to the location, donned his wet suit and examined the situation. The whale was safe because his blowhole was above the water line, but there was no way he could free himself on his own, without human help. Ted had an ingenious idea. He

Namu, the killer whale (© *MCMLXVI United Artists Corporation — All rights reserved*)

would build a cage underwater, around the killer whale, then free him of the net and tow him with a tugboat to Seattle. It was incredibly hard work to build a sturdy cage, without a top, that could withstand being towed three hundred miles. But Ted was up to the challenge, and the cage eventually began its voyage south. Ted christened the whale Namu, making the little fishing village famous.

Killer whales travel in schools and so Namu's family refused to leave him. They followed the tugboat at a safe distance while their relative was being taken away from the northern waters. Killer whales in this part of the world feed mostly on salmon, and it so happened that the salmon migration at this time of the year was moving in a northerly direction. So after a few days, the whales got hungry enough to abandon Namu and turn north in search of food.

When the contraption Ted built arrived in the Seattle harbor, I was there with my wife and three sons to observe the first captive killer whale in the history of zoology.

To me, Namu was a beautiful creature. His back was jet black, his belly was white; under his eyes he had white spectacles, and he did not look dangerous until he opened his mouth. His sharp triangular teeth were three times larger than the teeth of the great white shark, and with them he could have sliced a walrus or a polar bear in two. But he did not appear to be like a creature who would want to hurt anybody. The fish we threw to him remained untouched. We were worried at that time that he might starve to death. Ted engaged some fishermen to bring in live salmon, because he did not seem to have any interest in dead fish, as dolphins do.

All day I stood on the dock, watching the whale. When night fell, everyone left the caged animal, but I could not leave him. I sent my wife and children back to the hotel, and then I approached the whale. The cage was hung on giant timbers, and I just squatted down on the timber to be closer to Namu. Namu could have picked me off easily, but that thought never occurred to me. Then Namu swam to me and looked into my eyes. I felt that I was facing an intelligent creature. Then the idea came to me that Namu was not simply an animal but a visitor from another world, like the man on the Planet of the Apes. Namu was from Planet Sea, and we from Planet Earth were keeping him captive. We had cut him off from his family, wives, and children. He must feel lonely, depressed, hopeless about his fate. His giant skull contained a brain much larger than mine, and no one had yet told him that we did not plan to harm him, that we planned to love him, take care of him, learn from him, and that maybe one day we would let him go back to the North Pacific to rejoin his family and relatives.

I was thinking all this, when Namu started to make noises. The noises were not threatening. On the contrary, they sounded strange coming from such a massive creature. His voice was high pitched, and it reminded me of a cat's meow. Of course I knew that dolphins communicate at very high frequencies, not audible to the primitive human ear, and a killer whale is the largest species of the dolphin family, but the noises he made had still surprised me. I knew he was trying to talk to me, but I could not understand what he was saying.

To show my sympathy and interest in him and to ease his loneliness, I tried to imitate his high voice and answer him. My effort to express my inner feelings by being close to him and by making his kind of noises soon paid off. Namu stayed all night where I sat. My feet were hanging into the water, and he could have bitten them off at will, but I had no fear. I kept company with a lonely creature and the creature appreciated it. He hated to be alone, and a puny apelike man's presence meant something to him, otherwise he would have moved away. But he never did. As long as I was there, he was there, and we kept eye contact.

Many thoughts crossed my mind — about our prejudices against the unknown, our unwarranted fears of wild animals, our condemnation of a creature for eating other creatures to survive. What are we doing? Aren't we slaughtering thousands and thousands of cattle every day? Sheep, chickens, goats, turkeys, fuel our biological furnaces — and then we fear an animal who does the same thing that we are doing. Namu was so close now that I could touch him. I touched his wet skin and told him I was his friend.

Next morning Ted and I made a pact. We would make a film about a zoologist making friends with a killer whale. From here on, I would be responsible for any expenses involved. We planned to move Namu to a better place. We would film our experiences to try to bring the truth about killer whales to the general public.

During the next six months, we had incredible experiences with Namu as we filmed, both above the surface and underwater. The result was the first film about a killer whale.

When we towed Namu to Rich Cove, at the other side of Puget Sound, and placed a giant net around the cove to keep Namu within range of our cameras, Namu became much happier. Ted Griffin, in his wet suit, was the first man ever to approach a killer whale underwater. In a few days, he was able to get Namu to eat salmon out of his hand. My cameramen and divers were equally brave. Lamar Boren, my underwater cameraman who is three hundred pounds of muscle, became just as friendly with Namu as Ted Griffin was. Soon Ricou Browning joined us, and Namu felt even less lonely.

Once Namu began to eat, his appetite was enormous. He could consume between two hundred and four hundred pounds of salmon a day, a diet of fish worth many hundreds of dollars. He rejected all other food, including our swimmers. When anyone went rowing in our dinghy, Namu lifted the boat on his back and carried it along gleefully. In six months' time, he never dropped the boat. Soon everyone was swimming with Namu. Lamar Boren's attractive wife was riding on his back, as she might on a dolphin. All the killer whale acts we see today in the many Seaquariums and Marinelands originated in Rich Cove with Namu.

Soon several famous scientists joined us. Dr. Thomas Poulter came from the Stanford Research Institute and Dr. Ted

Walker arrived from Scripps to record Namu's vocalizations. We were learning a lot about killer whales as we made our film.

One day Ted and I made our mistake. The two of us decided that we had to capture a mate for our lonely bull. I allocated twenty-five thousand dollars for the expedition. I will never forget the hunt. Our plan was to locate a school of killer whales from a light plane or a helicopter, then chase a female close to shore where we could drop a mile-long and twenty-six-fathom-deep net from our large fishing boat to capture the female. This is how we planned it. Expert fishermen told us that killer whales can swim very fast but only for a short period of time.

Sighting the killer whales was not difficult. To chase them with a high-powered speedboat was also possible. There was one thing we could not do — chase them to waters less than twenty-six fathoms deep. Obviously, the killer whales understood our plan and knew that the nets would go down to the twenty-six fathom depth only. Thus, whenever the depth finder of the fishing boat indicated that we were very close to the limit, the killer whales turned and swam back under our boat to the open ocean. It turned out to be a lie that they tire fast and will slow down. They kept up their twenty-knot speed for hours.

The whole expedition reminded me of a World War II Navy picture. An American destroyer flotilla is chasing a German submarine. Whenever they think that they have her trapped, the German sub sneaks away, employing some great trick of deception. Soon I was rooting for the killer whales, betting against my own twenty-five thousand dollars.

But the battle was on, and no one could stop it. It was near dark. A female slowed down somewhat when her daughter became so exhausted that she could not keep up with the school. Then we shot a signal light into the female's blubber just behind the dorsal fin, where the whales are the least sensitive. Our flotilla pursued the signal light, and finally we succeeded in capturing the young female.

By means of tremendous effort and good logistics, we delivered the captive female to Namu in Rich Cove. Ted named the thirteen-foot girl Shamu, and we all believed that Namu would be thrilled to have a companion he could talk to and make love to. Unfortunately we were wrong. Namu and Shamu just did not get along. Namu was not interested in Shamu. He was more involved with the people around him: being hand fed by Ted, playing with our dinghy, swimming with human companions. Namu did not allow Shamu to approach him, and the few times she did, he became rough.

We were quite confused by this turn of events. Namu was often visited by other killer whales, who stayed on the outside of the net. One night, forty killer whales visited Namu, having picked up his sonar signals. We still do not know why Shamu was not accepted by Namu, but Ted speculated that Namu was too young to mate.

Sad as it was, we finally decided to sell Shamu to Sea World in San Diego. They constructed an excellent pool for Shamu and paid us twenty-five thousand dollars, her capture cost. The logistics of the transportation were quite spectacular. The Flying Tigers Airfreight provided a DC-7 cargo plane with a giant stretcher and overhead showers. The tail end of the plane could be opened at a ninety-degree angle for loading. A giant crane lifted the whale onto her stretcher for the five-hour flight. Thus, Shamu arrived in San Diego without any difficulty. She liked her new home and became the darling of the masses.

A few years later, I was in London when I heard that Shamu had attacked a girl who was riding on her back. I refused to believe it, and I was quite right not to. Shamu had been trained to pick up objects thrown into her pool and take them to her trainer. In this case, the girl riding on her slid off Shamu's back and fell into the water. Shamu, conditioned to retrieve, picked up the girl between her giant jaws without hurting her and carried her to the trainer. Of course the girl was scared to death, not understanding why she found herself in the jaws of a killer whale, but it was an act of playfulness rather than an act of aggression.

After meeting and loving Namu, I became quite interested in learning whether killer whales had ever attacked a human being. The old New England whalers were exposed to them all the time. Whaling ships were followed by killer whales because there were often scraps of whale meat left over for the killers. Reading the logs of many of those ships, I never found evidence that any sailor who fell in the water from their longboats or from the whaling ships was ever attacked or eaten by a killer whale. I did learn of a fairly recent incident near the California Channel Islands in which a diver, wearing his black rubber suit and black hood, was picked up in the jaws of a killer whale. Suddenly, however, the whale dropped him unharmed, realizing that he was not one of the seals or sea lions it was hunting.

There are many legends in Australia about killer whales who chased giant whales (among them a ninety-seven-foot blue whale) to the whaling ships. While the harpooned whales were hoisted to the deck, the killers tore big chunks out of the carcasses. The easy food had attracted them to the whalers. In Twofold Bay in Australia, some of the whalers just waited for certain smart killer whales to chase the finbacks and bowheads to their ships and dorys. Among those killers was the famous Old Tom, who assisted whalers for more than a hundred years, which indicates the longevity of the species.

Dr. Francis Charles Fraser, a retired curator of the British Museum of Natural History, used to tell me interesting stories about his Antarctic experiences. He said that killer whales would come up next to the ice floe where they were camping, and enjoyed having their backs rubbed with long brooms. (Namu, also, liked it when we brushed his back.) Killer whales, he observed, sometimes seem aggressive when they try to break up ice floes with people on them. After studying these individual cases, however, he found that those whales were only trying to get to the Eskimo dogs, which they mistook for seals, and not to the two-legged humans.

The killer whale is probably the most perfect creature of the sea. Nothing is stronger or faster in the water. Its white belly attracts fish life because all fish gather at places where there is light. The paddle shape of its pectoral fins allows the killer whale to turn faster than other underwater creatures. Killers survive equally well in tropical waters, such as Baja California, or in the icy-cold arctic currents. They feed on fish, seals, sea lions, sharks, and other whales, but in the northern Pacific, where we observed them, they eat salmon only. The whales follow the great salmon migrations and will feed on dolphins or seals only when they lose the migrating salmon in a storm.

Their giant brains are about six times larger than the human brain. They can use logic, they can communicate with each other, and they are both needful and smart. For instance, when we played with Namu and he was happy, he kept jumping high out of the water, but he never endangered anybody by coming down on human swimmers or capsizing our small boats. Namu, to me, was a great revelation about other levels of intelligence. His may be unlike ours, but it has to be respected.

Since our experience with Namu, many other killer whales have been captured, and their trainers have developed the same admiration for them. There is one warning I have to make. A giant creature in a limited environment cannot be totally happy. Sooner or later, depression or other neuroses may set in and may change a good-natured creature into a bitter angry specimen, just as solitary confinement does not improve the disposition of a human being. I am against keeping killer whales in captivity. The capture of Namu was coincidental. We have learned a lot since then. I would prefer that no more killer whales ever be captured and that no more whales ever be killed.

17　I, the Ape

I AM AN APE and know it. I am not ashamed of it, but I am not proud of it either. It would be much nicer to be a dolphin or a tiger or a leopard. Even house cats have more dignity and freedom than the human ape. Human apes are easily enslaved and have little pride. Cheetahs, house cats, leopards, can very rarely be enslaved or made to do things they do not want to do.

My first ape friend was a young orangutan I rented from Trader Horn's animal compound in Thousand Oaks when I was producing a science fiction TV film. This little male orang, born in Borneo, had the softest fur I have ever touched. He embraced me affectionately and loved me from the start. I was his new surrogate mother — his security blanket. His face so resembled the face of a human, his expressions were so loving and touching, that I suffered separation anxieties when I had to return him to his compound. On weekends I often drove out to visit him, and he always recognized me. I would take him on walks and give him piggyback rides. But then he grew into a giant and was moved to the Los Angeles Zoo. His baby face turned into the impassive mask that all adult male orangs have, and he no longer recognized me.

The next ape I made friends with was another actor in a science fiction film. I hired the same chimp that had played Cheetah, Tarzan's friend in all the Tarzan pictures. The chimp

Ivan Tors and a relative (*Bill Ray, Life Magazine,* © *1967 Time, Inc.*)

was no longer young and was not considered safe with people, so his keeper had to treat him roughly. An adult chimp can be very strong, mean, and stubborn. Human strength is no match for his. Still, the old chimp took to me at first sight and remained affectionate all through the filming. Sometimes he got mad at my prop man, broke away from his keeper, and climbed up to the rafters of our giant studio. It would take hours to retrieve him with bribes of oranges and bananas.

Chimps up to the age of six years are believed to be more intelligent than human children of comparable age, and the only reason they cannot talk is that they lack the proper vocal cords. At the Yerkes Regional Primate Research Center (a place I love to visit in Atlanta), chimps are trained to use sign language, to use a typewriter, to select the proper keys for opening different locks, and to use a computer for communication. They manifest skills within the human range.

Some anthropologists say that the reason they did not develop as far as humans is that the competing human apes chased them back from the open savanna into the forests and, as tree dwellers, they found it unnecessary to develop skills other than taking care of their young, climbing trees, swinging from one branch to another, finding food, establishing a rank order and copulating. In a troop of chimps in the wild, for instance, all members love and take care of the young. Because chimps are particularly fond of the young, kidnapping each others' babies is not uncommon, even if it is only for a short time.

Early in July of 1963, I was with Dr. Leakey, the discoverer of the missing link between prehumans and humans. We had dinner at the New Stanley Hotel in Nairobi, and he told me with great excitement that a young English woman was working for him, studying and living with chimps somewhere in Tanganyika. He showed me some snapshots of the handsome, tall woman and her chimps. Since then, the whole world has come to know Jane Goodall as the great pioneer of primate research. One of the snapshots showed a chimp sticking a reed into a termite mound in order to fish the termites out and eat them. It was the first photographic proof that chimps can use tools. Once this was established, behavioral science moved ahead with teaching chimps, until we now take it for granted that a chimp can manipulate a simple computer.

In 1965, we introduced a chimp named Judy to the *Daktari* series. Judy's popularity in this show matched that of Clarence the Cross-Eyed Lion and of the bear Gentle Ben. In fact, one could say that she became world famous. *Daktari* was the first American TV show purchased for Russian television. I was told that when *Daktari* was on the air, the streets of Moscow were empty. Everyone stayed at home to watch it, and Judy became the biggest attraction after the Bolshoi Ballet.

When we started working with Judy, she was a young, intelligent and affectionate chimp. (Not all of them are. I must emphasize again and again that the individual differences among animals are just as wide ranging as among humans. For instance, we owned a big male chimp, Chester. I am willing to sign an affidavit stating that Chester was the most stupid animal I ever had the misfortune to work with. He was not interested in learning, reward or no reward, and he died stupid.) Judy, on the other hand, turned into quite a miracle. While we were filming, she watched her trainer, Frank Lamping, keenly. She could obey around seventy-five hand signals, and she never held us up in shooting. Her great intelligence was made manifest, not by her ability to be trained easily, but by her adjusting herself to the technique of making films. She understood the essence of what she had to do in a shot although the director had no language with which to convey it to her.

For instance, in the film *Daktari*, the doctor, his daughter, and another actor were having tea on the porch of Daktari's house. In this shot, Judy lifted her cup and drank her tea with the others. After the long shot, which is when the camera photographs a whole group, we usually photograph each actor at a

Judy, the chimp of *Daktari* (*Metro-Goldwyn-Mayer*)

closer angle so that only one person or, in this case, one monkey can be seen. In these individual close shots, the actor has to continue to do what he or she was doing in the long shot — such as drinking tea — since otherwise the scenes cannot be properly put together in the editorial room. After a few shows, Judy fully understood the meaning of matching scenes. When they photographed her in a close-up, she did her act of picking up the cup and drinking exactly the same as she had done in the long shot. She understood clearly what was expected of her. When the assistant director signaled a lunch break on the set, the sound mixer tooted a horn, which indicated that everyone was to stop working and get in the chow line. Judy's reaction was immediate. When she heard the horn, she would drop her acting and line up with the actors for lunch. (I've seen the same behavior with working elephants, who were as aware of the signs and sounds of work breaks as their human keepers were.) Exactly one hour later, the sound man would toot his horn twice, meaning that everyone was to get back to work. Judy would be the first to return to the set and resume the same position or stance she had been in before lunch, understanding that the work would take up again where it had left off.

Dr. Tony Harthoorn, the world famous pioneer in the immobilization of wildlife, visited me at Africa USA with his wife, Sue. While we were having lunch, Judy pulled the shoelace out of one of my soft safari shoes — one of her favorite pastimes. I took my shoe off and told Judy to fix it. Dr. Harthoorn found it incredible that Judy was able to thread the shoelace back into my shoe. She also figured out how to pick locks and open the cages of other animals, and so we had to watch her carefully. She was filled with curiosity and, once she learned something, she utilized her knowledge.

Chimps have a natural fear of certain creatures, such as lions and snakes. Judy was intelligent enough to overcome these natural fears once she realized that these creatures meant no danger to her. She rode on elephants, had pillow fights with Clarence, and even rode on his back and led him on a leash. One inherent quality that remained intact, however, was her maternal instinct. When we introduced a baby chimp named Coco as an added character, Judy immediately picked her up, carried her, loved and protected her, as if Coco were her own child.

Judy also had some human faults. She was extremely jealous and demanded all the attention of the persons whom she cared for or who were important to her welfare. For instance, I was casting long-haired dogs for a part. About twenty owners brought their dogs to Africa USA. I selected an English sheep dog and began to play with him. Judy, who was observing this from the top of a tree, was fuming with jealousy. When she could not take it any longer, she leaped off the tree, landed behind the dog, tore a handful of fur out of his coat, and disappeared into the bush.

People often ask me why I think dolphins are superior to apes. I have a few answers. One of them is that dolphins, with their larger brains, understand their own strength. A child can swim and play with a dolphin. The three-hundred-pound mammal will frolic and jump around but will never touch or hurt a human. Judy did not understand her own strength. When she was an infant and weighed twenty to thirty pounds, she used to leap onto our backs from trees, and it was fun; but when she weighed seventy pounds and jumped on me from a high branch, she often injured my back. Another reason is that apes are destructive in captivity, while dolphins are not.

What primates and dolphins have in common is that both need a family. They are not loners. I witnessed in experimental laboratories that apes can be driven insane when separated from others and not touched or not cared for. They become autistic, schizophrenic, catatonic. They develop human mental diseases when isolated. Their posturing in isolation is almost identical to the posturing habits of seriously mentally ill humans. They repeat movements, such as turning their bodies or heads compulsively, all through their waking hours. It shows the very close relationship between the human primate and our African cousins.

I observed female chimps in their natural surroundings and found them to be excellent mothers. But a restricted, isolated chimp in a laboratory will not care for her young. She may drag her newborn on the ground by the umbilical cord, having failed to sever it. She will not pick up her infant or put it to her breast. However, a mentally sick chimp can be rehabilitated by placing it among normal chimps. Slowly it will pick up, by imitation, the more normal manners of the others and revert to near-normal chimp behavior. Only now and then will it revert to the posturing of the insane. Isolation will sicken a chimp, but reintroducing it into a chimp society will revitalize the animal. Unfortunately, we are doing the opposite with human primates. We separate the mentally ill from society rather than place them among normal people, where a patient could relearn communication with others.

Traveling around the world, seeing tribes, clans, and families of different nationalities, of different colors, I have found that the best mental health exists among people where the family ties are strong and loving, where the whole clan contributes to the mental well-being of the others. Only the witch doctors, shamans, *kahunas, curanderos,* are loners among them. (And it is by being very different that they can have such an hypnotic effect on their people.)

I feel better in Africa than anywhere else in the world. There I live in synchrony and harmony with nature. I wake with the sun and go to bed when the sun retires. I walk on soil, not concrete. I breathe pure air, oxygenated by photosynthesis and not fouled by gas, asbestos powder, and sulphuric acid mixtures, which eat away at our lungs, eyes, sinuses, throat, and anything exposed to them. In Africa I see life and death as they occur, for they are not hidden from me as they would be in a large city, where birth and death occur behind closed doors. We are also kept from seeing the slaughter of the animals we feed on. Nature is not always as it is shown on a Disney film for children or in *Flipper* or *Daktari*. Nature can be cruel. The predator eats the prey; the weak are consumed. But this strengthens the gene pool, for the strong and the healthy survive. We, on the other hand, may destroy the world by forcing the weak to survive. We may overpopulate the earth to an extent that famine and utter destruction of humanity may result. Nature is cruel, but it is realistic. Life in a big city thwarts real life forces. When in New York, I always feel like an ant or a termite, not a human. I lose my dignity. Perhaps the chimps and gorillas were lucky when they withdrew to their jungle and kept their families as their largest unit.

In Africa, I stopped being afraid of death and of dying. I accepted death as part of life, the way most natives accept it. Death has dignity, just as the struggle for survival is granted respect. They are interconnected. Once there is no struggle, life stops and we vegetate. I want to live only as long as I am useful. I do not understand people who cling to life. Africa and acquiring knowledge of my fellow primates have given me peace of mind and serenity as well as lowered my blood pressure and improved my health. (Whenever I return to a city, my blood pressure jumps twenty points.)

I have learned from primates how to be a good, loving parent; how to allow my children freedom as long as they are not endangered; how to keep close to them without hovering over them or interfering with their individual development. The young must learn from their own mistakes and develop along their own genetic paths. There is a rank order among primates: The strong rank higher than the weak or slow, and that's nature's way.

The rank order among primates is very interesting. When I lived with my young sons on the slope of Mount Kenya, the Safari Club maintained an animal orphanage. The actor Bill

Holden, who was co-owner of the club, contributed to the mé-
nage a chimpanzee born in captivity. The chimp, John-John,
was a great friend of my sons', and whenever my children
began to fight with each other, he became furious and tried to
break up the fight. He was on a fifty-foot chain, tied to a tree,
but even when the boys were beyond the range of his chain, he
would still try to break up the fight by throwing twigs and
stones at the aggressor. In his territory, protection and aggression were his privileges. Although born in captivity, he felt that
he was genetically the dominant one, and so disciplining
should be his right alone.

Among the observations I made while studying monkeys and
apes was my theory about their hysterical behavior. Primates
really have no physiological weapons to protect themselves
from fierce predators like leopards, tigers, hyenas, and other
large cats. Their teeth are not daggerlike and their nails are not
claws. When the average primate is attacked by a predator, the
predator usually wins. The female primates are often much
smaller than the males. On the average, the male's weight and
size is double that of the female's. When a troop of primates
sight an approaching predator, they are often at the predator's
mercy. All they can do is scream hysterically in their panic.
The uproar of these combined screams often frightens the
predator away. Based on this experience, the troops of females
learn that screaming is a good defense.

One of the many physical proofs that our ancestors were
apelike is that, although our large canine teeth have evolved to
their present size, the roots of our canine teeth are still much
larger than roots of our other teeth. If you touch the part of
your gums above your canines, you'll feel how much longer the
roots are there. Old Man Darwin knew what he was talking
about. Besides, the number of chromosomes we have is nearly
the same as a chimp's, with the chimp having two more chromosomes than we have. The Explorers Club studied a weird
chimplike creature named Oliver, whose appearance was half-

way between chimp and human. It turned out that this chimp had only one chromosome more than a human.

The ancestry of man can probably be traced to a tiny mammal called the tree shrew. The various offshoots of this tree-dwelling mammal arc most likely the grandparents of the present-day human. Our immediate predecessor was a creature about four feet tall and with long arms, who during the next three million years, grew to our present size. Our size is not constant. *Homo sapiens* is still evolving. If the ratio of growth from generation to generation continues at its present rate, we may end up as eight-foot people within a hundred fifty years. Of course, this growth may be the result of vitamins and good nutrition, and we may settle down at a certain size. From ancient armor, we can tell that five hundred years ago the average soldier was about five feet two inches tall. At the time, a six-footer was considered a giant.

I am five feet eleven, and when I arrived in California in 1940, I was considered particularly tall. Now all of my sons are inches taller than I am. This increasing growth in our species has to be reckoned with, for a bigger body needs more calories, and the food supply on our earth has a limit. The change in sizes in the animal world always had a lot to do with the available food supply.

The largest of the apes are the gorillas, and there are not many left in Africa. These peaceful, humanlike creatures were misunderstood for thousands of years. There are hundreds of film posters of fierce gorillas carrying off scantily clad, blond maidens. Nothing could be further from the truth. Such recent observers as Dr. George Schaller and Dian Fossey testify that gorillas are good-natured bands of wanderers, feeding on bamboo shoots at quite high altitudes, as they are pushed back farther by the pressures of the new agriculturalists. They try to avoid humans; they are good family creatures; and they like to avoid trouble by shimmying up high trees, carrying their young with them, when approached by humans. They will become extinct soon, for they do not adapt well to human pressures and do not breed easily in captivity. In the high mountains of Zaire and Ruanda, which are mostly of volcanic origin, we find the last of the mountain gorillas.

In the very wilds of West Africa, we find the lowland gorillas. The lowland gorillas are even worse off than the mountain gorillas, for they are forced by hunger to raid the banana trees of the plantations, and so they are usually killed and their young captured. The meat of the adults is eaten and the young are sold to the zoos of the world at incredibly high prices. I bought two lowland gorillas for Africa USA for $10,000, and I lavished on them everything that would make them comfortable. I built them a large hygienic enclosure. Their sleeping quarters had infrared heating. I assigned Pat Darby, the best-qualified nurse, to take care of them. The three-year-old was manageable, because she was too young to remember the cruelty of her capture. The five-year-old, however, was already ferocious, and it was too late for us to try to touch him or make close contact with him. We tried to bribe him with luscious fruit plates of walnuts, grapes, orange slices, and bananas, but still we could not tame him to a point where we could work with him. I did not, however, want to separate him from his sister; so eventually I made a trade with the Hawaii Zoo. I shipped the two gorillas to them in exchange for two young giraffes.

Since I needed a gorilla for a film we were making, I made contact with a family in Seattle that had a gorilla named Ivan as a pet in their household. Ivan was only two years old when he was introduced to me in my office at MGM Studios. He was a playful, cuddly thing who raised hell by climbing over my desk, tearing up scripts and memos. Finally, when he was exhausted, he fell asleep in my lap. When I took him out to my ranch, he quickly made friends with Judy (the chimp) and Prince (Helfer's German shepherd) and enjoyed freedom and nature without any shyness or caution. Ivan's muscles were already well developed, and the strength of a strong man was no match for him even then. Judy, who was six at that time, could not stand up to Ivan, and so she had to do whatever he wanted her to do. We finished a very funny film with Ivan and the other animals. The little gorilla, the chimp, and the German shepherd became inseparable friends and playmates. It was another example of interspecies attraction.

When we needed an adult gorilla for one of our films, we did not use an animal but an extraordinary athlete named Janos Prohaszka, who was a Hungarian movie stuntman with a circus background. He was a small man with extraordinary muscular development. He could climb up anything and was the true "human fly." He was also one of the very few athletes who could stand on one index finger. But, beyond this, he developed a specialty that Hollywood often found useful. He studied the behavior of chimps and gorillas, including the sounds they uttered. Then he created realistic gorilla and chimp suits that he could wear. In costume, with the proper posture and uttering the apelike sounds, he fooled many, many experts.

I once asked Janos, who had become my very good friend, if he would help me do a behavioral test with gorillas in the San Diego Zoo. Dr. Charles Schroeder, the founder and director of the San Diego Zoo, had given me permission to try an experiment. At the zoo, there were many realistically constructed gorilla compounds, each housing a gorilla family. I had asked Janos to dress up in his gorilla outfit, so I could test whether the big apes depend more on eyesight (as the human ape does) or on their sense of smell (as most other mammals do).

So one Sunday morning I walked with my fake gorilla, Janos, down the road toward the gorilla compounds. We were a good four hundred feet away from the first gorilla compound when pandemonium broke loose. The gorillas in the first compound had spotted the approaching human gorilla, and the sight of an intruding gorilla had frightened them all. This indicated to me, among other things, that gorillas are very territorial animals. The mothers, in a panic, grabbed their babies and stood behind the big, silver-backed male screaming hysterically. The male pounded his chest menacingly, ready to protect his harem and children.

The same scene repeated itself at each compound. Finally, Dr. Schroeder stopped the experiment, afraid that this condition of panic might hurt them. (A frightened female had tried to jump over the moat around her compound and had fallen into it — luckily without injury.) Our experiment at the San Diego Zoo indicated that gorillas do not differentiate between human scent and gorilla scent, and that they rely on the evidence of their eyes.

Janos Prohaszka, and his twenty-four-year-old son died soon after that experiment. Wolper Productions was producing a documentary on the evolution of the apes, and Janos and his son were dressed in costumes to portray different prehistoric apemen. Their plane, going from the location site to Los Angeles, crashed into a mountain in the Sierra Nevadas.

Janos's costumes are still being used in movies today. I certainly will never forget the friend who could so mimic the apes — climbing trees, swinging from branches, uttering their cries.

18 Postscript

I LEARNED IN NATURE that everything is connected to everything else. For example, tides are connected to the gravitational pull of the moon. The grunion would not be able to mate without the aid of the tides. She lays her eggs in the sand on the beach when the tide is at its highest, so that for two weeks her eggs will not be washed back into the sea. By the next high tide, her young will be viable and safe.

To prove the cosmic interconnection, I enter an empty room and make it dark. If I bring in a short-wave radio, I can hear the whole world, from police calls and pilot talk, to music performed by the Vienna Symphony or by Alice Cooper. If I turn off the radio and bring in my portable television set, through satellite transmission I can watch the finals at Wimbledon or the Bolshoi Ballet. But, now, if a jet flies over the empty room, at a height of, say, twenty thousand feet, the TV image is suddenly distorted. What happened? The energy field surrounding the high-flying jet interfered with the energy field of my television set, and the messages became scrambled. I turn off the TV set and bring in a simple instrument called the Wilson Cloud Chamber, invented at least sixty years ago. It is only a translucent tube filled with vapor. While observing the vapor, I discover the appearance of fast streaks, not unlike the contrails that high-flying jets leave behind in the cold clean air of the stratosphere. What causes these fast, straight streaks in the cloud chamber? The answer: cosmic particles, electrons, protons, neutrons, and other subatomic particles that bombard the earth constantly, attracted by the gravitational pull of our massive but small planet. Without the "magic" chamber, this traffic of basic particles would be invisible, although it is responsible for mutations in genes, birth defects, and variations in development.

There are no empty rooms or empty places on this earth. A cobweb of cosmic communication surrounds us. We are caught in it, we live in it. We are plugged into the cosmos — past, future, and present. We are plugged into each other and into each living thing. We are whirled around by energy forces responsible for lasers and masers, electromagnetic radiation, DNA and RNA, until a double helix of amino acid unwinds and life begins. All life originated from a single DNA molecule probably created when lightning passed through primordial methane gas. All living things on this earth have one common ancestor, and that first organic molecule ties us all together. All the cells in our bodies, all the cells in each living creature's body, have common memories going back a few billion years. Some cells remained one-cell organisms like the amoeba. Some survived, some were devoured by a group of cells that joined forces for the purpose of attack or common defense. For each opportunity, different groups of cells evolved. The fit survived, the unfit were consumed by the fit. The differentiation of cells and cell groups continued for billions of years. The result: simple organisms in the oceans, from diatoms to jellyfish, skates, rays, fish. Then some climbed out of the sea and became reptiles, the great saurians.

Much later still, evolution began to experiment with man, but today man is only at the beginning of his development. The end is not yet clear. Strangely, we, who are so different, are related to every life form. We have the same memories hidden in our chromosomes, and we can replay them in our dreams and fantasies.

A cosmic energy created the life force that urges us to copulate, to propagate, to improve, to repeat. All creatures are variations on the same theme. We are tied to the shark, tied to the birds; we are tied to the tiger and tied to the frog by an invisible but very real cord. Lying on top of my sleeping bag, looking at the southern sky where the Milky Way is the only superhighway in sight, listening to the many tones and sounds of the tropical night . . . suddenly I understand this kinship. I can reach out to touch the sky, touch the trees, and touch the animals around me.

But although I have tried, I cannot find words to express how I truly feel in nature. So here I must stop.